PARADISE LOST AND FOUND

MAINSTREAM / SPORT

PARADISE LOST AND FOUND

THE STORY OF BELFAST CELTIC

PADRAIG COYLE

MAINSTREAM
PUBLISHING
EDINBURGH AND LONDON

To Jane, Matthew, Patrick and Hannah —
the best team in the world

First published in Great Britain in 1999 by
MAINSTREAM PUBLISHING COMPANY (EDINBURGH) LTD
7 Albany Street
Edinburgh EH1 3UG

This edition 2001

ISBN 1 84018 451 5

A catalogue record for this book is available from the British Library

Typeset in Garamond and Peignot Demi
Printed and bound in Great Britain by Cox and Wyman Ltd

CONTENTS

Acknowledgements

Thanks to all those who allowed me access to their memories, photographs and personal papers so that this story could be written. Inevitably, there will be factual inaccuracies in the dates and times of some events. I hope this doesn't distil, too much, the spirit of the grand old team.

Oswald Bailie; Jonathon Bardon; Joan Bevington; Bob Bryson; Jackie Cummings; Jim Delargy; Johnny Denver; Paddy Devlin; Jimmy Donnelly; Dr Sean Fulton; Edward Grant; Ron Greenwood; George Hazlett; Frank Hennessey; Colin Jones; Jimmy Jones; Will Lunn; Roberta Maguire; Stephen Maguire; Tom Matthews; Roma McAlinden; Myna McAlinden; Bobby McAuley; Sean McCann; Michael McGuigan; Bill McKavanagh; David McKavanagh; Danny McKavanagh; Charles McLoughlin; Jim McSparran; Malachy McSparran; Annette McWilliams; Mick McWilliams; Sean Mooney; Alex Moore; Kevin Murphy; Vincent O'Brien, Liverpool FC; Mick O'Flanagan; Dr Eamon Phoenix; Patricia Redfearn; Billy Scott; Edward Sears; and Charlie Vernon.

Thanks also to:
Belfast Central Library; Linenhall Library, Belfast; S.E. Education and Library Service, Ballynahinch; *Northern Whig; Irish News; Belfast Newsletter; Belfast Telegraph.*

Photographs courtesy of Jimmy Jones, Sean Mooney, Danny McKavanagh, Frank Hennessey, Alan Markley, Meekin & Anderson, and *Irish Independent Newspapers.*

ONE

DEATH OF A LEGEND

On a sharp winter's day on 17 December 1996, mourners gathered at First Holywood Presbyterian Church for the funeral service of 84-year-old Harry Walker, one of the town's elder statesmen whose death, three days earlier, had been unexpected. His final resting place was in Redburn Cemetery close to the ninth green at Holywood Golf Club where, as it happened, his grip on life was finally released. It was a fitting end to a life so dominated by sport that, even after the ageing process had insisted that he hang up his football boots, he continued with a pursuit which offered a competitive challenge.

Harry Walker had been one of the giants of the Irish League, where his most successful years were as a player with Belfast Celtic. It was a tribute to his reputation that the funeral service was attended by so many outside the family circle.

One of the mourners asked the Walker family if he could bring a wreath of green, white and orange flowers – the symbol of unity between Irish nationalist and Ulster unionist – into the service. The family agreed. At the graveside another mourner confided that he had contemplated removing his green and white football scarf which he was wearing under his trench coat and throwing it on top of the coffin.

'I've had this Belfast Celtic scarf for over 50 years. It's the most precious Celtic possession I have,' he told John Walker, Harry Walker's son. 'Your father was a real legend. He epitomised what Belfast Celtic stood for. I thought that this would be the most sincere way of expressing my respect for him, but I didn't want to offend your family.'

'Why didn't you?' replied John Walker. 'You could not have paid him a bigger tribute. We wish you had.'

John realised after he left that the man had gone without giving his name.

What, in sporting terms, can be said to constitute a legend? If the following suggested definitions are accepted – a modern-day phenomenon which has been absorbed into local folklore; an individual or team whose fame or notoriety continues to generate tales of exaggerated or romanticised exploits – then Belfast Celtic Football Club – like Walker himself – most certainly falls into that semantically over-used category.

Take a journey along the Falls Road in West Belfast and the evidence is hard to ignore. Amongst green, saffron and white flags, the political slogans and the gable-end graffiti emerges the story of a football team like no other, a team whose symbolism and meaning for an entire community has never been erased by the ever-shifting political, social and architectural landscape of this deprived and troubled inner-city area. In this part of Belfast, football is a way of life. In almost every one of its narrow, terraced streets, knots of young boys and girls can be spotted kicking a ball around, with as much fervour and self-belief as at Wembley on FA Cup final day. Local support for clubs like Manchester United, Liverpool and, especially, Glasgow Celtic, is clear from the names emblazoned on the back of their replica shirts – Beckham, Giggs, Owen, Larsson, Donnelly . . . When these kids get a ball at their feet, they really become, in their imagination, their footballing heroes.

Yet for all the tabloid fame and huge spending power that 1990s' sporting super-stardom brings, today's game and its top players cannot hold a candle to the profound and lasting effects that Belfast Celtic wrought on the community that nurtured and believed in it.

For these young footballers of the future, Belfast Celtic is now little more than just a name. But for their parents, grandparents and great-grandparents, the belief in the status of the team is undiminished. It is 50 years since Celtic departed the Irish League, after one of the most dramatic and shocking incidents in Irish football history. And although the numbers who can claim to have seen its players in action may be in steady decline, its former players grown old, its enormous achievements have passed down through family generations and into the folklore of Catholic nationalist West Belfast.

There was much to enrich that folklore. In its 58 years of

existence, Belfast Celtic were crowned Irish League champions 14 times. In doing so the club scored more than 1,800 goals while conceding an estimated 950 goals in 700 League matches. Belfast Celtic's dominance of Irish football was evidenced by the other honours they brought to Celtic Park, which included eight Irish Cups, eleven City Cups and ten Gold Cups. In 1940, the team played 36 games without defeat and in a seven-month run from the end of August 1947 to March 1948, Belfast Celtic won 31 consecutive matches.

The mystique was enhanced by the missing years when Belfast Celtic dropped out of football, leaving its supporters and the Irish League to wait patiently for the club's return. During the First World War the Irish League was suspended from 1915 to 1919 and, on its resumption, Celtic won the Championship. Then it disappeared again for four years, due mainly to the civil unrest of the 1920s.

These were turbulent years in Irish history as civil war and partition of the island led to serious violence and murder, particularly in Belfast.

In 1924–5 Celtic were back and their unaltered run continued until the 1948–9 season when the club departed for the final time. That last act had been precipitated by a riot which occurred at the end of the derby game at Linfield on Boxing Day 1948, when a mob attacked several of the Celtic players. The most seriously injured was centre-forward Jimmy Jones who had his right leg deliberately smashed. As the crowds dwindled away from that game, little did they realise that the days of Belfast Celtic were drawing to a close.

Towards the end of the season the Irish League was informed of the club's decision to withdraw from football. Celtic embarked on what turned out to be a farewell tour to North America, representing Ireland in an international series. And the club departed in style with six victories, two draws and two defeats in the ten-match programme. The most satisfying result of all was the famous 2–0 win against Scotland, the British champions, at Triborough Stadium, Randall's Island, New York, on 29 May 1949.

It was thought that Belfast Celtic's decision would be short-term and that the club would eventually return. But it never did. In the intervening years there have been many theories as to why that was the case.

The club wanted justice for the way in which it had been treated.

The sanctions imposed by the Irish Football Association against Linfield following the Boxing Day riot were paltry. A one-month closure of the ground and a reversal of Linfield's fixtures did not match the severity of the attack on Celtic's players. Of all the disputes the club had with the football authorities down the years, this was the most formidable and Belfast Celtic felt let down by the authorities.

There have since been suggestions of a power struggle amongst board members over the direction the club was taking in its financial interests: it was run as a very successful business, accumulating wealth through transfer deals and gate receipts and heavy investment in the facilities at Celtic Park. There was some unease at the introduction of greyhound racing to the stadium as well as resistance to the attempts by some directors to increase their shareholding.

There was also the belief that, as a new political landscape was beginning to emerge in Belfast following the Second World War, nationalists had started to feel increasingly isolated within the Northern Ireland state. The Boxing Day riot may have served to reinforce the view that the blight of sectarianism was not going to go away and that Belfast Celtic would continue to be the focus of civil unrest.

Could it be that the old order represented by Belfast Celtic was starting to become outdated and that the board considered the team's era to be coming to an end? It might just be that Belfast Celtic did intend to return, but as the years slipped by, the impetus to come back into the fold was lost. It was a decision which left the Celtic faithful in a state of mourning. The Irish League and Celtic's rivals also lived to regret the club's departure. Attendances and gate receipts fell and the atmosphere surrounding football in Belfast was never quite the same again.

TWO

HUMBLE BEGINNINGS

The intensity and passion with which Belfast embraced the coming of association football was little different from that in other cities throughout Britain. Glasgow, which has maintained industrial and social links with Belfast for generations, played a part in its genesis. Of all the people who might, eventually, have brought the game to Ireland, the first person to take the initiative was John McCredy McAlery, a Belfast drapery merchant, who witnessed football being played while out walking with his new bride during their honeymoon in Glasgow.

McAlery, who would later captain Ireland in its first international – a 13–0 defeat by England – invited Queen's Park and Caledonians to Belfast to play an exhibition match at the Ulster and Windsor Rugby Football Club on the Ormeau Road on 24 October 1878. He followed up that enterprising venture by encouraging the formation of several clubs including, in 1879, his own Cliftonville Association FC.

The Irish Football Association was founded at a meeting at the Queen's Hotel, Belfast, on the evening of 18 November 1880. A Major Spencer Chichester was elected its first president with John McAlery being appointed secretary. McAlery recorded in the minutes that '. . . if the spirit which pervaded those present be acted upon, the result will be a strong association for promoting the game which we have espoused.' Of the inaugural seven clubs only two, Cliftonville and Distillery – the first professional side in Ireland – remain.

In 1890, the year before Belfast Celtic was born, the Irish League established itself to organise the game on a similar basis to that of England. At that stage Linfield, who would become Belfast Celtic's greatest and most bitter rivals, was already in existence and showing itself to be a powerful force in Irish football.

The game was spreading throughout the island. Dublin's teams included Bohemians, Dublin Association and Dublin University. With some financial assistance from the Irish FA in Belfast, the Leinster FA was formed in October 1892 as the number of affiliated teams in the capital city rose to five. The Munster FA was established in Cork while, nearer to the Irish FA's Belfast headquarters, the County Antrim FA came into being.

The growth in popularity of association football in Belfast needs to be judged against the social and political conditions of the city as it prepared for the advent of the new century amid the uncertainty that the union with Britain would be maintained. Extreme forces, which were already feeding the fears and prejudices of a mostly uneducated population, would continue to do so. For some, allegiance to a particular football club would also come to be seen as loyalty to a religious or political cause. To opponents, that made them marked men.

Belfast in the 1880s was playing a major part in Britain's industrial development. The city, which is situated at the mouth of the River Lagan and Belfast Lough, had grown as a market town and port since the early seventeenth century. Catholics first went there as cattle traders selling beef in the Markets district and settling in a part of the lower Falls district which became known as the Pound Loney.

The river and its tributaries were a source of power for the textile mills, which developed in the 1770s for the processing of cotton. When the cotton market collapsed in the 1830s, the mills continued to operate by switching to the spinning of linen, which was a mainly female-intensive industry. By 1900 there were 60,000 women employed in the linen mills, meeting the world demand for clothes and the finery of the rich.

Other industries, including shipbuilding, engineering, rope works and iron foundries sought their space on the land between the steep hills to the east and west overlooking Belfast. At one time the shipyards were the biggest in the world, employing 25,000 men.

Yet, for all the economic prosperity of the city, the working classes lived in conditions of dreadful poverty. The life expectancy for women was 40; low wages, appalling working conditions and deficient diet encouraged the spread of infectious diseases; those employed in the linen mills were constantly working in a damp environment; housing suffered from inadequate sanitation and ventilation and, among large families living in cramped conditions, tuberculosis and typhoid spread with rapid and deadly effect.

Sectarian tension between the communities had ample opportunity to express itself long before football arrived in the city and it continued in parallel with Belfast's industrial success. The minority Catholic population had been welcomed and supported by their Protestant neighbours when they began to settle there in the eighteenth and early part of the nineteenth centuries. In the decades that followed the Great Famine of the mid-1840s, migration from the countryside into the city accelerated and, as competition increased for jobs and houses, so too did the level of intolerance. During the early years of the 1890s, 25 per cent of the population was estimated as being Catholic. By the turn of the century this figure dropped again as the overall population of the city expanded further.

There was serious rioting during August 1864 which was believed to have been caused as a result of the influx of Catholics who had come to work as navvies in the docks, where the sea approaches had been deepened to allow ships entry into Belfast port in all tides. There were clashes with the mainly Protestant shipwrights. The new Catholic and Protestant settlers brought their rural traditions and disputes with them into their own districts. And as invisible border lines were frequently crossed, continual territorial battles were fought in areas such as the Brickfields which lay between the mainly Catholic Falls Road and Protestant Shankill Road. These clashes were reminiscent of the activities of the Peep o' Day Boys and the Defenders – Protestant and Catholic gangs who used to confront each other regularly in sectarian warfare in County Armagh. The Peep o' Day Boys were the forerunners of the Orange Order.

Disturbances often took place on Saturday and Sunday afternoons when the mills were closed and alcohol was readily available. Engaging in a bit of communal conflict was one method of letting off steam. Perhaps it is no coincidence, then, that in the decades to follow, another place where battles over territory could be fought on Saturday afternoons would be the football ground.

The civil strife of 1864, and again in 1872 – was surpassed by the communal rioting of 1886, which was triggered by the defeat at the Westminster Parliament of the Liberal Government's first Home Rule Bill. Between June and September, over fifty people died in clashes between loyalists and nationalists on the streets of Belfast and in the shipyards. The rise of Irish nationalism was unnerving Protestants, who feared that the campaign for an Irish Parliament in Dublin, led by the politician Charles Parnell, would signal the end of the union between Ireland and Britain.

William Gladstone was determined to introduce a second Home Rule Bill and even before he had been re-elected to government, an Ulster Unionist convention was organised in Belfast's Botanic Gardens to protest against the plan.

Meanwhile, among those politicians visiting Belfast was Lord Randolph Churchill, who aligned the Conservative Party with the Protestant Orange Order and agitated its members to resist change. The fiery Presbyterian minister, Rev. Hugh Hanna, was one of several well known Protestant clerics whose anti-Catholic rhetoric fuelled sectarian unrest.

As news emerged from London that the second Home Rule Bill had been passed through Parliament, rioters again took to the streets of Belfast. Several of the city's leading industrialists were prepared to relocate their businesses to Glasgow and Liverpool in the event of Home Rule being granted.

Amongst Catholics there was to be a gradual religious renewal and political awakening. While the Reform Acts of the 1880s gave Catholic men the vote for the first time, influence and power within that community rested with a tiny, educated middle-class element comprised of priests, businessmen and solicitors. The Catholic Church had been unable to respond to the rapid industrialisation of Belfast and because of a shortage of priests to minister to the growing Catholic population, many rarely practised the faith into which they were born.

Bishop Patrick Dorrian of the diocese of Down and Connor, which included Belfast, led a mission crusade in 1865 to restore religious devotion. Within seven years, an estimated 70,000 Catholics were regularly attending services. The Church became a central pillar in the lives of these people. The clerics were seen as the natural leaders and the informers of opinion. They looked after the spiritual welfare of a poverty-stricken population and guarded against the keenly-felt intrusion of Protestantism. Little was done to bring down the barriers of mistrust and hatred which the communities felt towards each other.

In order to present the working-class people with some other outlets for their leisure time, the Catholic Church in Belfast and Derry encouraged the playing and support of football and boxing. These sports were easy to organise and suited the inner city environment. The Church also regarded football as a remedy against the militant republicanism which would come to be associated with the Gaelic Athletic Association. The GAA had been formed in 1884 to promote Irish cultural activities, including the speaking of Irish and the playing of Gaelic football and hurling. While these activities would take hold in rural Ireland, soccer proved to be a much stronger force in the cities and Belfast Celtic would come to represent the aspirations of the nationalist community in Belfast.

THREE

Belfast Celtic is Born

Belfast Celtic was formed in 1891 by a group of men from the Falls Road district of the city who saw the potential for a stronger team if the footballing talents in the local area including those from the local junior clubs – Clondara and Millvale – were to be amalgamated. Their wish, too, was to style the club on Glasgow Celtic both in the way it played and its charitable work off the field. When secretary Bob Hayes wrote to the Glasgow club, the financial donation that Belfast Celtic received in return added to the initial subscriptions of nine shillings raised at the inaugural meeting.

The club did not gain entry to the Irish League until 1896 and spent those formative seasons establishing itself in the ranks of the Irish Junior Alliance. It won the Robinson and Cleaver Shield at the first attempt and retained the trophy for the next two seasons. In those three seasons Celtic lost only two games in 50 matches and went through the 1894–5 League campaign unbeaten. Belfast Celtic's growing reputation was enhanced further by its performances against senior opposition. In 1893 it defeated senior club Cliftonville to reach the final of the County Antrim Shield where it lost to Distillery. Belfast Celtic were runners-up again the following season before claiming the trophy in 1895 with a 3–1 defeat of Distillery at Solitude.

Once senior status had been granted, Belfast Celtic took a short time to acclimatise to its new surroundings. The club was without a permanent base and, in that first season in senior football, it had to play all its matches away from home. The club finished bottom of the Irish League in 1896-7. This was to be the only occasion when it would prop up the League and as Ireland moved into the new century, Belfast Celtic were crowned champions for the first time.

That successful side was built around defender Jimmy Connor

from Downpatrick, centre-forward Pat McAuley – who was the first Celtic player to be capped at international level – and winger Joe Abrahams who joined the club from Partick Thistle.

Those associated with the club realised that if it was to achieve its potential, it would need to be organised on a more business-like basis and on Friday, 19 July 1901, the first board of directors of The Belfast Celtic Football and Athletic Company Limited registered the new company according to the requirements of the Companies Act. The registration required the club to add 'Belfast' to the title because Glasgow Celtic was already a registered name.

The Memorandum of Association noted that the objects for which the company was established included the provision of:

> . . . a Football Ground and Cycling Track at or near Belfast, in the County of the City of Belfast, and to lay out and prepare such ground for Football, Cricket, Cycling, Athletic Games, Matches, or Exercises, and other purposes of the Company; and to provide Stands, Pavilions, Stages, Lavatories, Refreshment Rooms, and other accommodation and conveniences in connection herewith respectively.

While the company was keen to promote all these sports and to host competitions, it also declared an interest in acquiring land for property development and agricultural use, and to become involved in the wine, spirits and drinks trade. This was hardly surprising since the majority of its directors were spirit merchants, one of the few businesses in Belfast where Catholics were able to succeed.

In keeping with its wish to provide charity and welfare where it could – the club donated £100 to a local hospital when it won the first Charity Shield in 1904 – Belfast Celtic Football and Athletic Company formally set out how it proposed to assist those inside and outside the club who needed help. The club was:

> . . . to provide for the welfare of persons in the employment of the Company, or formerly in their employment, or in that of their predecessors, the Celtic Football Club, or any other Club or Association in which the Company may have

been or may be interested, and the widows and children of such persons and others dependent upon them, by granting money or pensions, providing schools, reading rooms, places of recreation, or subscribing to sick or benefit clubs, hospitals, associations or societies, or otherwise as the Company shall think fit.

To establish or support, or aid, or contribute moneys to the establishment or support of public hospitals or charitable institutions, or of associations, institutions, or conveniences, calculated to benefit shareholders of the Company or persons employed by the Company, or having dealings with the Company, and to give, subscribe, or guarantee money for charitable or benevolent objects, or for any exhibition, or any public, general, or useful object.

The initial capital of the company was £3,000 which was divided into shares of £1 each and the directors each took 10 shares. Their names, occupations and addresses were listed with the company solicitor, P.S. Brady of 25 Chichester Street, Belfast, as follows:

James Millar, Manager, Glenshesk, The Glen, Limestone Road, Belfast.
John McKenna, Mineral Water Manufacturer, Bath Place, Belfast.
David McCloskey, Brewers' Agent, Antrimville, Belfast.
John Rooney, Spirit Merchant, 16 Rosemary Street, Belfast.
Hugh Fitzpatrick, Spirit Merchant, 69 Leeson Street, Belfast.
Charles Watters, Draper, 134 Divis Street, Belfast.
Henry Scullion, Spirit Merchant, 112 York Street, Belfast.
Patrick McCreesh, Spirit Merchant, 78 Stanhope Street, Belfast.

The share capital of the company was established along the same lines as those used by the Quaker, Rowntree and Cadbury family businesses, in which the primacy and the voice of the small shareholder was to be promoted and protected as much as possible. Voting rights were deliberately weighted so that anyone amassing a large block of shares could not use that position to pervert the interests of the community, the members of which were the owners and the original subscribers. This meant that although an individual or group might hold a majority of shares, they would not have a controlling interest.

The first 15 shares entitled the owner to 15 votes. The next 10 shares added two extra votes as did the next 20 shares. Those with 55 shares had 20 votes.

A similar share-ownership scheme already operated at the *Irish News* morning newspaper. It was established in the same year as Belfast Celtic, with the support of the Catholic Church. Those involved in Belfast Celtic belonged to an emerging, ambitious Catholic middle-class business group which was starting to assert itself in the city. Men with entrepreneurial skills tended to gravitate towards trade, especially in wine and spirits, because there was little opportunity for advancement in the professions. By the end of the nineteenth century, most of the large public houses and hotels in and around Belfast were owned by Catholics.

The exodus from the countryside to the city during the nineteenth century had been assisted in no small way by the arrival of the railways from the 1840s onwards. Hundreds of young men with little chance of prosperity on the small farms in counties Cavan and Leitrim arrived straight off the Great Northern line into Belfast. Many of them found work in bars and pubs belonging to others who had taken the same journey long before them. After years of hard graft, they graduated to become publicans in their own right.

Those men who put Belfast Celtic on a firm business footing were joined by many others including Catholic priests who were prepared to buy shares in the enterprise. During the playing life of the club, up to 1949, it would be given long service by three dedicated chairmen, Dan McCann (1904–23), Hugh McAlinden (1923–38) and Austin Donnelly (1938–49).

Dan McCann was a poultry and fish merchant who also served on the board of the *Irish News*. He had an interest in politics and acted as election agent for Joe Devlin when he won the West Belfast seat by 16 votes in 1906. He was a founder member of the National Club which was based in Berry Street, a venue regularly used for Belfast Celtic board meetings. Hugh McAlinden's family were well established bookmakers. He took over the helm in 1923, a year before Belfast Celtic returned to football. He was regarded as a charitable man with a good temperament and head for business. One journal wrote of him:

He is a past president of the Irish League and in the Belfast
Charities Football competition he is a leading figure and
invariably presides over their deliberations where, at the
finish, if there are any odd sums, he quietly draws on the
cheque book to make them even – he considers it easier to
distribute £200 than £183.

Although Hugh McAlinden died in January 1938, the family
association with the board and playing staff of Belfast Celtic
continued. Austin Donnelly, who had brought the team back from
Irish League exile in 1924 and managed the club for five successful
years, succeeded Hugh McAlinden as chairman. He oversaw the last
part of the club's remarkable history and would be instrumental in
the decision to withdraw membership for good in 1949.

The club's search for permanent premises of its own resulted in
the purchase of some ten acres of land near the Falls Road end of
Donegall Road and folklore has it that the directors imposed an
unwritten agreement that shareholders would not be paid any
dividend until the ground was properly equipped.

In those early years it was accepted that a great deal of work
needed to be done to develop the facilities at Celtic Park and that,
since football would not be a paying proposition by itself, extra
revenue would have to be generated from elsewhere to meet the
costs of running a first-class team and to carry out improvements to
the enclosure and grounds. A variety of sidelines helped finance
those improvements. In 1903 the club installed a cinder track
around the playing pitch which was to be used for trotting races,
cycling events and athletics meetings. The first trotting meeting was
held there in Easter 1903. Some years later, meetings were staged
on Christmas Day to provide entertainment during the holiday
period. In 1925 Belfast Celtic agreed to co-operate with the
recently formed Northern Trotting Club at Lambeg, which was
eager for the joint promotion of the sport. That same year the club
secretary, Robert Barr, was commissioned to have a medal struck for
'Mr J. Lynch whose horse had lowered the track record for a mile
to 2 minutes 17 seconds at the Easter meeting'.

Trotting was a regular feature at Celtic Park until January 1927
when the track was re-turfed for greyhound meetings. The
forerunner to this activity may have been the whippet racing which

began in 1911. During the 18 years in which it was staged at Paradise, some of the meetings would attract as many as 200 racing dogs. In later years when it was noted that entries for the whippet meetings were falling off, one can only speculate as to the cause by the following reference in the club minutes: 'Various ways and means to improve the position were discussed and it was recommended that the services of one of the officials whose actions were deemed suspicious should be dispensed with at these meetings.'

Open-air boxing was promoted during the summer months. The first shows began in 1908 and continued until 1914. These were revived again after the First World War. The Celtic Park Easter Holiday Sports in April 1920 offered a six-hour card starting at 12.30 p.m. on both days for a combined entrance price of three shillings. The sports on offer included trotting, whippet races and five boxing matches – some of which were scheduled to go 15 rounds. The prize money for the trotting and whippet racing was £50 each. The club also made its facilities available for athletics and cycling meetings. The annual Celtic Sprint used to attract sprinters from all over Ireland and Britain. The presence of the world-renowned Arthur Duffey of the US at one of the meetings caught the imagination of the city.

Duffey, a graduate of Georgetown College, was a small man who won various college titles in the US and set several world records in the 100-yards sprint at the turn of the twentieth century, including a time of 9.6 seconds at a meeting at the Berkeley Oval in New York in 1902. He had been favourite to win gold at the 1900 Paris Olympics, but pulled up injured while leading in the final. All his records were subsequently erased in a dispute with James Sullivan, the founder of the Amateur Athletics Union. Sullivan, a former baseball star, had a successful sports goods business and the clash between the two arose when Duffey refused to wear Spalding running shoes. In 1905, allegations and counter claims were being made that Duffey was accepting money from a rival manufacturer to wear its equipment. For his part, Duffey threatened to expose others who were breaking the amateur code.

While those were issues that were to emerge subsequently, it is clear that Duffey was acknowledged as a sports superstar in his day and that his participation at an athletics meeting in Belfast in the summer of 1903 would have been a major public attraction. In the

Georgetown College Journal, Duffey's recollections of his visit to Celtic Park remarked on the huge crowds and the wet weather. He wrote:

> The journey to Belfast was a wearisome one, and though the crossing takes but a few hours, it was the roughest passage one would care to take. Arriving in Belfast after a bad attack of seasickness, I summoned up courage enough to meet the Irish runners the next day. Unfortunately the day proved a most unsuitable one for sports, yet in spite of the torrents of rain which fell incessantly throughout the day, great crowds of Irish enthusiasts were present to see the Irish Booth-Hall Sprint. Fearing that the cold day and the muddy track would defeat me, I picked my way through the preliminary heats and though tired and drenched to the skin, in the final I gradually wore down my opponents and won on the tape in 10 seconds, breaking the Irish record. Never shall I forget the mad rush of the spectators on the field previous to the final heat. Their enthusiasm knew no bounds, and though the committee and police made great efforts to keep them back, we finally raced with the people lined up on both sides of the track and finish, so that after I hit the worsted I was totally engulfed by the surging mob, and only with great trouble did I succeed in getting safely to the dressing-room. With the unpleasant prospect before me of recrossing the Irish Sea, that night I left the 'Ould Sod' and made my way to Bolton, England, racing there on the Monday. Though in fine form in this race, I was outclassed, owing to the poor condition of the track and the handicaps I was conceding.

While Arthur Duffey's memories of the running surface at Celtic Park were less than complimentary, the track was found to be suitable for plenty of other events. Belfast Celtic's secretary, Robert Barr, was a former champion cyclist and he persuaded the board to permit racing to be staged on the track. On occasions the Irish Road Club held its 25-miles championships at Celtic Park.

In 1905 Celtic Park was the first ground in Ireland to have covered accommodation in the unreserved area. The corrugated roof lasted many years before being blown down in a storm. Twenty years later, the purchase of the adjoining Willowbank Estate allowed for the expansion and improvement of the unreserved area. Someone even thought to landscape the outside of the banking which supported the terracing with flowers and shrubs. The blending of their fragrance with the balm of liniment must have created a pungent aroma in the garden of Paradise.

The money was raised through an overdraft facility with the Munster & Leinster Bank and the sale, by public auction, of properties at Alameda Terrace recouped part of the outlay. Consultations regarding the more expensive construction of a covered unreserved stand on the Willowbank side of the ground got underway in March 1925 with the appointment of Messrs F. & J. Wardle as architects. That firm was directed to investigate the suitability of a number of steel girders on sale at Bangor station. The costings for the new stand were put out to tender and after due consideration the contract for the steel work went to Redpath Brown Ltd, Glasgow, for £4,320 14s 8d. The building work was granted to Messrs Carson & Sons, Belfast, at a price of £4,328 7s 3d.

The new 5,000-seater stand was completed in 1926 at a cost of £10,000. That year, the company recorded a net profit of £94 12s 5d which might explain why the board, on receiving estimates of £154 for additional urinals and £54 for brick walls at the end of the new stands, decided not to proceed with this work. In October 1926 an extra charge of three pence was added for admission to the grandstand.

But that was not the end of the spending on Celtic Park. Work continued on improving the playing surface which, in the wet winter months, would turn into a mud bath. It took four years to gradually replace the clay soil with a substantial depth of sand and turf. By 1935, Celtic Park boasted one of the best playing surfaces in Britain and players were discouraged from walking on the pitch during training sessions. It is even reported that the groundsman was so protective of the playing surface that wooden planks had to be placed on the grass to allow the ball to be retrieved. Local boys were recruited, and paid, to weed the playing surface. The ground capacity eventually reached more than 60,000. There was, however, a serious setback in August 1938 when a large portion of the reserved stand was destroyed by fire.

Belfast Celtic's relationship with the Irish Football Association was a turbulent one. Apart from the club's assertion that the Irish FA failed to act honourably in the wake of the assault on Jimmy Jones by Linfield supporters on Boxing Day 1948, there were numerous other arguments down the years. Issues such as crowd behaviour, player suspensions, the format of competitions and even the size of the goal posts prompted the frank exchange of views between the club and the relevant football authorities. The club felt that Paradise was not being used enough by the Irish FA to stage both international and cup matches. There were suggestions that it would pull out in 1907–8, but it did not go through with that threat.

The following season the Irish FA's Rough Play Commission suspended Celtic and Cliftonville in the wake of trouble at a Charity Cup match. Both clubs contemplated withdrawal from football and only retracted their letters of resignation when those suspensions were lifted. The ten-month suspension of centre-forward Neal Clarke in April 1910 led to more problems. Crowd trouble and the intimidation of the referee in the game against Bohemians at Celtic Park brought further punishment – the closure of Paradise for one month. Celtic regarded this as unjustified compared to the treatment being meted out to other clubs for similar offences. The directors and shareholders supported a move to withdraw, but the Irish FA, realising the potential loss of revenue to the local game, was forced to reconsider its decision.

For a brief time during 1912, Belfast Celtic and several other clubs broke away from the Irish FA in a disagreement concerning the allocation of gate receipts from matches.

The dissenting clubs organised their own cup competition which became known as the Gold Cup. The dispute ended in a settlement between the clubs and the Irish FA.

In those early years of the new century, Belfast Celtic realised the business potential of selling players to cross-Channel clubs. First to be transferred was full-back Billy Clay who was sold to Sheffield United in 1903. The Yorkshire city would return for three more players, Andrew Hunter, Peter O'Connell and Paul Warren in 1909. Mickey Hamill is regarded as the first of the great Celtic heroes. Starting his career as an inside-forward, he played for the club in 1909 before being transferred to Manchester United for £175. Thousands of supporters turned out to bid him farewell at the railway station. In 1913 Celtic Park staged a match between Bradford and Manchester United of the English First Division. It was arranged as part of the transfers of Louis Bookman and Mickey Hamill to Valley Parade and Old Trafford. A large crowd watched Bradford win 2–1.

Hamill, who would hold the rare distinction of winning Championship medals in Ireland, England and Scotland, returned to Belfast before moving to Glasgow Celtic for a season. Belfast Celtic's withdrawal from the Irish League in August 1920 left Hamill and several other players unemployed: they were attached to Celtic but had no competitions to play in. Eventually, at the end of September, Hamill returned to Manchester after Celtic negotiated with his former club, Manchester United, and he signed for Manchester City at a price of £2,000. At Maine Road he played as a centre-half. Hamill captained Ireland to its first Home International Championship in 1914. He took his skills to America where he played for Forth River in Massachusetts and he finished his playing career back at Paradise. It was noted in the minutes of October 1926 that Hamill had returned to Belfast and that the club should check on his availability. During the meeting of 16 October the following was recorded: 'Lengthy discussion on the possibility of signing Mickey Hamill who had lately returned from the US. Mr Hamill was called in and explained his position. It was eventually decided that the chairman and secretary should go to Manchester on the 19th and interview the City club directors.'

Hamill rejoined the club and was to win three consecutive championship medals before retiring to manage his own aptly titled 'Centre Half Bar' on the Falls Road. Sadly, his life ended in tragic circumstances in July 1943 when he was found drowned in the River Lagan.

One of Celtic's best known supporters was the nationalist politician Joe Devlin who found favour with both sides of the community because of his continual efforts to confront sectarianism and to improve the conditions of the unrepresented working class in Belfast's industries.

Devlin did not play for Belfast Celtic, but there was an undeniable link between the two. Celtic's rise to great heights was mirrored by the popular support and devotion which spanned Devlin's political career.

'If you were a Devlinite who came from a fairly traditional Falls Road background, you supported Home Rule, conservative politics and Belfast Celtic. That wasn't mixed with the GAA and the Gaelic League which had republicanism behind them,' explains Dr Eamon Phoenix, the Belfast historian who has researched the impact of Joe Devlin's life on West Belfast.

'Devlin had a great memory and oratorical skills. His parents could not afford to send him for elocution lessons so he used to practise in front of the mirror making great speeches from Shakespeare. Lloyd George described him as the greatest orator of his day.'

Joe Devlin was born into a poverty-stricken background in Hamill Street in 1871 and grew up in the shadow of St Peter's pro-Cathedral. His father was a jarvey who owned his own cart and would hire himself out. Joe went to St Mary's Christian Brothers School, Barrack Street. In later life, when he became an established politician, he created several Joe Devlin bursaries for academic achievement at the school. These provided working-class boys with the opportunity for advancement. The scheme continued in the 1960s.

The sectarian riots of the 1880s caused by the Home Rule debate had a major impact on Devlin. His home in Alexandra Street West was close to the major flash points that separated the Falls from the Shankill and the violence he witnessed, as Belfast spilt along orange and green lines, convinced him of the need to pursue a non-sectarian philosophy. During the 1880s Joe Devlin got a job working in Kelly's Cellars, a pub in Bank Street. He was promoted to manager and during that period was introduced to the idea of Home Rule politics by the pub's owner, Sir Samuel Young, the Protestant nationalist MP for County Cavan.

When the *Irish News* was set up in 1891 as the main nationalist newspaper, Devlin moved to a white collar occupation as a junior reporter. In 1897, he left the *Irish News* to establish his own weekly newspaper, the *Northern Star*, because of his opposition to the influence of Bishop Henry of the Down and Connor diocese, who had gained control of the *Irish News* four years earlier.

'Bishop Henry believed that politics should revolve around a clericalist axis headed by himself,' says Dr Eamon Phoenix. 'He established the Belfast Catholic Association which was composed mainly of upper-middle-class Catholic doctors and lawyers to represent the interests of Catholics in the Belfast Corporation. Bishop Henry selected the candidates himself and in Joe Devlin's opinion this clerical interference in politics confirmed the worst Orange assessment of the sectarian nature of nationalist politics.'

Devlin regarded Henry as a divisive force which was preventing the Irish Parliamentary Party from establishing its roots in the growing Catholic community in west and north Belfast. He also felt that Bishop Henry was equating nationalism with Catholicism.

At the same time, Devlin realised that the Catholic vote in Ulster needed to be harnessed into a unifying force behind the campaign for Home Rule and he set about reorganising the Ancient Order of Hibernians which had existed in the rural counties of Armagh, Cavan, Tyrone, Fermanagh and Donegal since the 1790s under various titles such as the Defenders and the Ribbon Men. Though Devlin knew it to be a secret Catholic sectarian society which paralleled the Orange Order, he realised its potential as a bonding force for the nationalist vote at a time when the political allegiances in Ulster were equally divided.

'Devlin believed that he could blend together the Ulster Catholic small farmer and the Belfast Catholic worker in a Home Rule movement. It could become the green cement to counter the orange cement which held Unionism together,' explains Dr Eamon Phoenix.

However, Devlin failed to recognise that the AOH, of which he became grand master in 1905, frightened Protestants and made it difficult for them to identify with nationalism and the quest for Home Rule. Hibernian parades and processions were seen as mirror images of the tribal sectarianism of the Orange Order and, while support came from many clerics including Bishop Patrick O'Donnell of Raphoe, others such as Cardinal Michael Logue described the movement as 'a pest and cruelly tyrannical'.

Joe Devlin was encouraged to pursue a political career at

Westminister by a group of publicans, merchants, retailers and solicitors which included Dan McCann, Hugh McAlinden and Richard Byrne. These people realised that the Catholic population was almost totally voiceless and that 'wee Joe' was the person to represent them. In the 1906 general election, Devlin, with Dan McCann as his agent, won the West Belfast seat by 16 votes.

FOUR

THE POT STARTS TO BOIL

There was no reason why football should have escaped the effects of the political events that were destined to divide Ireland two decades into the new century. As the storm clouds began to gather over Europe, Celtic embarked on the first ever continental tour by an Irish club. The visit to Bohemia, in 1912, ended with one defeat from the six games played.

Back in Ireland the clouds were darkening, too, as another Home Rule Bill was introduced by Prime Minister Asquith. Winston Churchill had already been to Belfast in January of that year to promote the bill. His public meeting was switched to Celtic Park with the help of Joe Devlin, when it was discovered that unionist protesters had blocked the Ulster Hall. One report of the gathering said that apart from the speeches, 'Among other things the event was memorable for the number of empty wallets and purses afterwards found in the ground.'

While nationalists held the expectation that on this occasion it would be third time lucky for Home Rule, unionist opposition to the move was manifested by a huge public demonstration on Saturday, 28 September 1912 at which an estimated 200,000 loyalists signed the Ulster Covenant. In the build up to what was to become 'Ulster Day', Linfield visited Celtic Park on Saturday, 14 September for a League game that was abandoned because of crowd trouble which erupted at half-time. The Belfast morning newspapers reported the events in different ways.

The *Irish News* on Monday, 16 September wrote: 'The tuition of Sir Edward Carson and the gospel of hatred so zealously expounded in the Belfast Unionist Clubs have so far affected the minds of their dupes that even the arena of sport is not considered sacred from mob violence.'

It then explained that the violence had been unexpected, but as 20,000 spectators packed into the ground long before the game got underway, tensions rose. While Celtic and Linfield supporters cheered their teams, a gang at the Donegall Road end of the ground seemed to be there solely to incite others by flying Orange bannerettes and crying anti-Pope chants. When the trouble flared at half-time, stones and bricks were thrown and a man with a revolver was seen to take careful aim and fire into the Celtic support.

The *Belfast Newsletter* described the game as being spoiled by 'a regrettable disturbance between the respective partisans of the two clubs'. It reported that the trouble had broken out when Celtic supporters unfurled a green and white flag which carried the slogan 'Play up Celtic' and proceeded to taunt Linfield supporters. The *Newsletter* view of the shooting incident was that: 'A young man from behind the judges box fired a revolver in the direction of the Linfield crowd.' Luckily no one was killed although an estimated 60 people were injured and taken to the various hospitals. No arrests were made.

Although the *Ireland Saturday Night* newspaper appeared to credit the points to Linfield who led at the time, the game was not played to a finish. The *Northern Whig* felt that the game should be regarded as unfinished and be replayed at a 'neutral venue', if there was such a thing. The game was eventually replayed in mid-week a month later without incident. In November the clubs met again at Windsor Park where the echo of gunfire drowned out the sound of the referee's whistle as Celtic saw four goals being disallowed. Linfield won the game.

The following year the Ulster Volunteer Force was mobilised by Dublin lawyer Sir Edward Carson and, on the eve of the Great War, it armed itself with guns that had been smuggled into the country through Larne harbour. A nationalist army was also raised under the Wexford barrister John Redmond, who supported Home Rule. He believed that the cause would be furthered if Irishmen fought for England in the 1914–8 war.

While loyalist and nationalist fought side by side in the trenches of northern France, militant republicans led by school-teacher Padraig Pearce orchestrated an uprising in Dublin in Easter 1916. Defeat was inevitable and initial public hostility turned into support of the rebels' campaign for an Irish Republic, when the British military authorities executed 16 of the leaders involved in the insurrection.

The island was on the road to partition and the eventual formation of the new state of Northern Ireland, but not before much blood was shed in a violent campaign by the IRA. Belfast would not be immune from the brutality as sectarian confrontation affected the city once more.

Against that backdrop, the Irish League was suspended from 1915 to 1919 as it became clear that the war in Europe was not going to be easily won. The Belfast and District League was formed though Belfast Celtic chose not to enter. Instead, a reserve side took part in the Intermediate League, winning it in 1917 and 1918. And the club finally claimed the Irish Cup at the fourth attempt 12 years after its first appearance against Shelbourne in 1906. After losing to Linfield and Glentoran in 1915 and 1917, Belfast Celtic finally made the breakthrough in 1918 with a 2-0 victory against Linfield in the second replay at Grosvenor Park where Norman Stewart scored both goals. The team that afternoon was: Elisha Scott, Willie McStay, Fred Barrett, Jimmy Mulligan, Mickey Hamill, Norman Stewart, Danny McKinney, Jackie McIlroy, Jimmy Ferris, Herbie Johnston and Harry Frazer. Willie McStay was a soldier who had been posted to Belfast. He was suspended from the Irish League for a period when he went home on leave and played a game for his former club, Glasgow Celtic, without permission.

In the first post-war season, Belfast Celtic were winners of the one-off Belfast and District League in 1919 and when the Irish League Championship resumed, Celtic wrapped that up, too, with three points to spare over Distillery. Within six months, however, Belfast Celtic was to disappear into voluntary exile. The board of directors under the chairmanship of Dan McCann explained that in the present dangerous circumstances it felt unable to put either its players or supporters at risk in travelling to other grounds. Those were the days when in particular, the Oval, Glentoran's ground, which lay in the shadow of the shipyards, had a reputation for identifying Belfast Celtic supporters for later attack. Anyone showing visible support for the club would be assumed to be a Catholic and could, unknowingly, have their coat marked with chalk. As they made their way home through the infamous Dee Street that led from the Oval, they would be set upon by Protestant adversaries. In the turmoil of political uncertainty, it is not surprising that the rivalry and sectarianism of perceived enemies would be aggravated further when working-class people were corralled together in great numbers in the same football ground on a Saturday afternoon.

While rugby union was able to retain its all-Ireland dimension, soccer administration on the island fragmented and, by the time the Irish Football Association realised what was happening, it was too late to prevent the formation of the Football League of the Irish Free State in 1921. The seeds of mistrust were sown in the final years of the nineteenth century as the Dublin clubs, determined to make their contribution to the growth of the game, began to sense that the international selectors were ignoring their players in favour of those attached to northern clubs. Dublin did not stage an international game until St Patrick's Day, 1900, when 10,000 people watched Ireland lose 2–0 to England at Lansdowne Road. That same year Dalymount Park, the home of Bohemians, was opened. In years to come it would rival Belfast's Celtic Park and Windsor Park for atmosphere. Only when a Dublin club could lay its hands on the Irish Cup would the city feel that it was fully integrated into football in Ireland. The Freebooters from Sandymount and Shelbourne were beaten finalists before Shelbourne conquered Belfast Celtic 2–0 in 1906 to bring the first major trophy south. Bohemians won the Irish Cup in 1908 against Shelbourne. The Dublin clubs felt that those achievements were worthy of greater recognition at international level, but their sense of scepticism was never to depart.

The Easter Rebellion of April 1916, the Anglo–Irish War and the Irish Civil War that followed were the wedges that were eventually to push the football bodies, north and south, apart.

Tensions began to rise again in post-war Belfast. The economy was in a boom period as the Harland and Wolff shipyard worked to a full order book. But the Irish question remained unresolved and thousands of ex-soldiers, whose diet of violence in the trenches had left them perfectly prepared to give armed support to a political cause, were back in Belfast looking for employment.

On 6 March 1920, the Irish Cup semi-final between Belfast Celtic and Glentoran was played in Dublin and went to a replay following a 1–1 draw. A week later the sides met again, this time in a Gold Cup game at the Oval which Glentoran won easily 2–0. The only problems were created by Glentoran supporters who threw stones and struck one of the match officials. The referee halted the game until Glentoran stewards had dealt with the situation. Four days later, on St Patrick's Day, the Irish Cup semi-final replay was staged at Solitude and had to be abandoned ten minutes from time when crowd trouble occurred following the dismissal of Celtic defender Fred Barrett by referee William McLean.

This *Irish News* report of 18 March 1920 records how one incident turned a dour, scrappy cup game into an out-and-out riot.

> Wild scenes and incidents of a serious character resulted from the Irish Cup semi-final tie replay at Cliftonville yesterday afternoon, when the match had to be abandoned owing to a section of the crowd rushing on to the pitch and, in the subsequent disturbance when the opposing crowds came into collision, a revolver was used, bringing about a serious riot. There were repeated baton charges by the police inside and outside the enclosure and fierce stone throwing by the rival mobs, the entire disturbance lasting over an hour.
>
> Either three or four persons were subsequently treated for bullet wounds at the Mater Hospital, and at the same institution half a dozen others suffering from scalp wounds and fractures were admitted – a total of twelve, several of whom were detained for treatment.
>
> Save for singing and flag-waving by a crowd of youths congregated underneath the unreserved covering, the match had been without incident up to about ten minutes from the finish. This crowd sang various choruses, but had been orderly and no attempt was made to invade the enclosure. At the interval the referee had about a dozen youths, who were sitting inside the enclosure palings, cleared back to their original vantage points.
>
> No score had been recorded in the game and matters were quite normal when the referee ordered Barrett, the Celtic back, to the pavilion for apparently tripping Gowdy, the Glentoran centre-forward, when the latter passed him. The official was within his rights, but the offence looked to be a very simple one of a common type, occurring scores of

times in hard-fought games. Play had been perfectly clean and without any serious fouls, both sides playing strenuously, and no fooling had entered up to this point.

Immediately Barrett was sent off, a spectator rushed across the field and attempted to assault the referee. There was a struggle and the crowd commenced to rush to the scene. The referee at once went towards the pavilion and the players followed without molestation. The police had rushed to the official's rescue and he reached the pavilion uninjured.

The incident might have ended here but for a fusillade of stone-throwing from a section of the crowd at the unreserved exit. A rush was made in their direction by the crowd, which had invaded the field, and a wild scene followed.

Revolver Shooting.

In the mêlée, a couple of revolver shots rang out, one of those on the playing pitch evidently having opened fire in the direction of the opposing stone-throwing crowd. A stampede occurred, and in the rush for safety a portion of the ground palings was torn down, through which the crowd made a very hurried exit.

Several additional shots were fired and the police rushed in the direction of the shots. A man fled towards the Waterworks side of the enclosure, but was rounded-up by a large body of police and taken into custody.

He was at once handcuffed and kept in the centre of the ground, surrounded by a body of police some 50 or 60 strong. The police charged with drawn batons and scattered the crowd on the playing pitch with ease, the latter jumping the palings.

A second charge was made in the direction of the opposition stone-throwing mob outside, and the latter scattered in all directions, chased by the police, through the wasteland outside. The police returned after scattering the rioters, but a crowd of several thousands remained in the ground for safety – the reserved standites retaining their seats.

The prisoner still remained guarded in the centre of the pitch, and the police made a further clearance of those inside the railings. In this clearance several persons were severely batoned and bore traces of injuries as they jumped over the railings.

Up to this stage, it may be said, the situation had been very effectively handled by the police, but later it did not seem necessary to use batons when orders were given to get the crowd in the reserved side outside. The latter were not a disorderly mob, being apparently merely those who had remained for safety.

Among those to receive treatment for their injuries at the nearby Mater Hospital were 14-year-old Patrick Murphy from Whiteabbey who remained unconscious with a fractured skull; 27-year-old Royal Flying Corps airman David Wilson from Coleraine who had been knocked over in the stampede; and RIC man, Sergeant Michael Lavelle of Donegall Pass Barracks, who had a bullet wound under the chin.

The police did make two arrests: 19-year-old George Goodman from Quadrant Street was alleged to have fired the revolver and later charged with attempted murder, while Hugh McVittie from the Newtownards Road was arrested on a charge of indecent behaviour.

The *Belfast Newsletter*'s coverage of the violence attributed much of the blame on the shoulders of Sinn Fein.

A disgraceful outburst by Sinn Feiners brought to an abrupt end the football match between Belfast Celtic and Glentoran at the Cliftonville Club's ground yesterday afternoon.

Peaceful persuasion on the part of officials of both clubs and the constabulary was unavailing and the police eventually had to make a series of baton charges . . .

Prior to the outburst the Sinn Feiners had been making their presence felt by singing the 'Soldiers Song', 'A Nation Once Again' and a parody on a well known Orange ballad, in which they introduced insulting references to the King.

By the time the Irish FA Senior Protests and Appeals Committee met two days later in private session at Wellington Chambers to deliberate over the events of St Patrick's Day, Belfast Celtic had already lodged a protest. It objected to Glentoran's inclusion of McIlveen whose name, as was required, had not appeared on the list submitted for the Cup tie. The Committee found this to be so and Glentoran were expelled from the competition, in accordance with the rule. Having taken evidence from the referee and other witnesses, it was decided to remove Celtic as well.

The IFA's Emergency Committee had also gathered to consider the Solitude riot and ruled:

1   That the expenses for making good the damage done to the Cliftonville ground on the occasion of the replayed Irish Cup semi-final on 17 March, when ascertained, be deducted from the proportion of receipts payable to Belfast Celtic.

2   That, having heard the evidence tendered to the Senior Clubs Protest and Appeals Committee at a meeting tonight in connection with the replay and the opinions of the official witnesses of Belfast Celtic given at said meeting, and having considered the circumstances under which similar scenes occurred, the Committee are unanimously of the opinion that the Belfast Celtic FC be suspended from taking part in Association football under the jurisdiction of the IFA Ltd, until the matter is further considered at a special meeting of the Council in Committee to be held on Tuesday, 13 March.

Belfast Celtic was both stunned and angered at the punishment and in a letter to the Irish FA secretary Charles Watson, Bob Barr pointed out that while the club recognised that there were troublesome elements within its support, the Celtic directors took exception to the manner in which the decisions had been made and how Celtic's image and reputation had been tarnished by events at a neutral venue, which was not under their control.

> Your drastic decisions . . . seek to impose on our club a liability which we must repudiate and to identify our club and officials with conduct of spectators which we have always endeavoured by every means in our power to suppress.

Belfast Celtic was so indignant about what it felt was the complete lack of natural justice, that it made clear its intentions if the matter was not resolved to its satisfaction. Bob Barr's letter concluded:

> While my directors are satisfied of the soundness of the legal advice they have received, they would be very reluctant indeed to be compelled to resort to legal proceedings in order to right the wrong which has been done to them and put themselves right with the football public; but if your Association is determined to adhere to its decisions, we fear no other course will remain open to us but to have ourselves justified before another tribunal.
>
> Before taking such a step, however, I have been instructed by my directors to request you to rescind the several resolutions all of which we are advised are unauthorised and *ultra vires* that is to say:- (1) to rescind the resolutions removing Belfast Celtic from the Challenge Cup Competition (2) to remove *ab initio* the suspension of Belfast Celtic from taking part in Association Football (3) to pay my club their proper proportion of the Gate Receipts of the Cup semi-final of 17 March, without any deductions from same in respect of the damage to Cliftonville ground.

The Irish FA appeared unmoved by Belfast Celtic's letter and upheld the findings of its investigations. The matter was eventually settled out of court several months later by which time Celtic had withdrawn from the Irish League.

As to the 1920 Irish Cup, it was awarded to Shelbourne by default though Glentoran felt very aggrieved at the manner in which it was dumped out of the competition. The club wrote to the newspapers to make it known that a written request had been received from Belfast Celtic, before the semi-final replay, to permit the inclusion of the unlisted Thomas Mulholland in the Celtic team. Glentoran had agreed to waive any objection, though as it happened, Mulholland did not play.

Glentoran accepted that it had committed a technical offence by not listing McIlveen, but regarded Celtic's objection as unsporting. McIlveen, a replacement for Emerson who had withdrawn shortly before the game, played for less than three minutes before retiring from the game because of an injury.

Glentoran also took the opportunity to let it be known that, some seasons earlier in a cup semi-final, Celtic had failed to provide a list, but that it (Glentoran) had chosen not to take advantage of the situation.

Robert Barr reacted with indignation to these public statements from Glentoran and wrote to the *Newsletter* to inform them that he had no knowledge of the incident in a previous Cup semi-final where his club had not supplied a list. As to the present situation, he stated that no written reply had been received from Glentoran in regard to the status of the unlisted Mulholland. Barr informed the *Newsletter* that he had accidentally met the Glentoran secretary Mr Scott and received a verbal intimation that while the Glentoran directors might not object to Mulholland, it was common knowledge that he was not on the list and others might object. As a result, Mulholland was not included in the team.

Within a few weeks, Glentoran was embroiled in another incident when crowd trouble broke out at a match in Dublin against Shelbourne. The Glentoran players were locked in the pavilion for over an hour until it was safe enough to leave.

This incident provided the *Irish News* football correspondent, 'The Celt', with the ammunition he needed to launch a stinging attack on the Irish FA.

> Contrast the treatment meted out to Celtic and to Shelbourne. At Shelbourne ground a referee is brutally beaten so badly that next day he is scarcely able to walk. The Glentoran team are prisoners for an hour or more. A steward has his head split and a Glentoran player is smashed up with a stone.

Is the Shelbourne club suspended? Not likely. Oh, no. Is the club prevented from playing in Dublin? Not likely. Oh, no. The same crowd can watch Shelbourne in Dublin and beat another referee if they desire during the fortnight the ground is closed. Yes, certainly; why not? Any other club can use Shelbourne's ground during the fortnight it is closed. Yes, certainly; why not?

The article asked why Celtic were suspended and removed from the Irish Cup when none of these things happened in the game at Solitude. There appeared to be some amusement that while the Irish FA had, on the advice of legal consul, rescinded the decision that Celtic pay for the damage done at Solitude, other illegal actions might be discovered as a result of an impending writ to be issued in the Chancery Division of the High Court in Dublin.

Celtic's suspension from football lasted a month and it returned to action on 17 April 1920 losing 1–0 to Linfield in a trouble-free City Cup match at Paradise.

The following week as Celtic were crushing Cliftonville 9–0 in one of the Charity Cup semi-finals being staged at Windsor Park, Solitude was yet again the scene of disturbances when the other semi-final between Distillery and Linfield was abandoned with eight minutes remaining. In the subsequent investigation, the IFA held that the referee Mr Saunderson, who claimed that he was being stoned, had no grounds for abandoning the match and suspended him until January 1921.

With tongue in cheek, 'The Celt' asked in his column: 'Surely there are no other rowdies in supporters other than Celtic?'

Celtic were back at Solitude on 1 May to win their second trophy of the season with a 3–0 win over Distillery in the Charity Cup final. Thomas Mulholland scored the first goal after 20 seconds before the Belfast High Sheriff, Councillor W.G. Tomer JP, who kicked off the game, had left the field.

The season came to a close with Celtic playing out a 1–1 draw at Glenavon on Saturday 15 May where Jimmy Ferris's goal was the last that Celtic would score in senior football for another four years.

Boxing replaced football on the Saturday afternoons of the close season at Celtic Park. Other clubs, Glentoran, Distillery and Glenavon had also taken to promoting boxing contests, but Paradise had a faithful support which supported the shows as it waited for the football to return. The first inkling that Celtic were to withdraw from the Irish League was reported in the *Athletic News* on Monday, 24 May 1920, which stated that the Celtic directors had decided to close down football and had already issued circulars to English and Scottish clubs regarding the availability of Mickey Hamill, Fred Barrett, Bert Mehaffey and Jimmy Ferris. At the annual meeting in June, the issue would be brought before the club shareholders for further consultation. The first indication that the Irish League had of Celtic's plans emerged at its AGM on Friday, 28 May when a letter from Bob Barr was read.

> I beg to notify you that my directors have decided that, having regard to the recent events in football, they will not undertake the responsibility of running a team next season, and have referred the matter to our annual meeting, which will be held next month. In view of this decision it would be impossible for me to allow my name to go forward as a candidate for the Presidency of your League.

On Wednesday, 9 June 1920, that special meeting of Belfast Celtic Football and Athletic Co., Ltd was held at the Lecture Hall in the National Club, Berry Street. Chairman Dan McCann JP, explained that the purpose of the meeting was to consider the company's position regarding the promoting of football as a result of the directors' decision not to run a team during season 1920–1. The chairman outlined the board's views to the large group of Celtic supporters, but the final decision was to be made by the shareholders. Following a lengthy discussion, the following resolution was unanimously adopted:

> That this meeting shares with the directors of the Celtic Club the deep resentment which they and those whom they represent have received; and that, while recognising the justifiable indignation that inspired them to retire from the game, we respectfully urge, in view of the strong representations and the pressure brought to bear

upon them by other clubs, that they should reconsider their decision. In urging this course upon the directors in the interests of the sport, in which the Celtic Club has played so powerful and effective a part, we trust that in continuing football their generous action will be reciprocated.

The directors met afterwards and acceded to the request of the shareholders that the club remain in football. A delegation from the senior clubs had also met with the Celtic directors the night before the meeting to ask the club to reconsider. This had also softened the attitude of the Celtic board. And when the annual meeting of the Irish League re-convened, Bob Barr became League president.

The court action against the Irish FA was held in the Chancery Division, Dublin on Monday, 14 June where the Master of Rolls granted both parties orders of discovery.

By mid-summer it became obvious that Belfast's downward spiral into violence was going to have a consequence on Celtic's involvement in the game. The mass expulsion of Catholics from the shipyards and other factories on 21 July left many of the men of the Falls Road unemployed and with no visible means of support. Over twenty people were killed in disturbances in the city before the end of August and as the new season approached, Celtic was asking itself how it could possibly operate in such a climate. There was the element of safety to be considered for Celtic players and spectators, and there were the financial implications of trying to run a business in a community where there was little income.

Football clubs in Dublin were also becoming extremely anxious about the situation in Belfast. Undoubtedly their fears were being added to by the first-hand accounts of the terror from refugees of the pogroms and there was growing agitation against continuing in the Irish League.

The Irish League Management Committee met on Monday, 16 August to consider matters relating to the future of football that season and held its discussions in private before adjourning until the Friday of that week. But it was already common knowledge that Celtic would not be playing football and that a proposed friendly game with Cliftonville for 21 August was off. It emerged from the reconvened Irish League meeting on Friday, 20 August that

Bohemians, Shelbourne and Celtic had asked to withdraw from the Gold Cup and that the start of the League competition was being postponed.

Relief organisations were trying to aid the thousands of workers expelled from the work places. The fund was added to by £100-donations from Belfast and Glasgow Celtic. A benefit game was organised at Celtic Park, in October, for the dependents of people killed in the pogroms.

In the absence of Irish League football, the Falls League was inaugurated on Saturday, 16 October with the purpose of providing an outlet for the district until better times returned. It did not affiliate to the Irish FA.

Junior side, St James Gate, decided to join with Shelbourne and Bohemians in not playing League games in the North, though these three did agree to continue in the Irish Cup. The Irish FA took a stance that it would be too dangerous for northern teams to play in Dublin during the civil unrest there. The path to football partition took another step when St James Gate refused to defend the Intermediate Cup which it won in 1920. Gate felt that this was the only course of action it could take on learning that the Irish FA had reversed a decision to play the 1921 Intermediate Cup final in Dublin. The overall situation went from bad to worse when Glentoran and Shelbourne played a draw in the 1921 Irish Cup. The venue for the replay should have been Dublin, but when the Irish FA ordered Shelbourne to return to Belfast, it refused.

The Leinster FA took the view that since the two cities were becoming more and more isolated from one another, the 'best interests of football might be served by severing its ties with the Irish FA.' A circular was sent around the Dublin clubs seeking their attitudes on the matter. The Leinster FA pointed out that if it were given a free hand to organise its own affairs, more could be done to popularise the game. Clubs were advised that the consequences of such an action would be ineligibility to play in the Irish FA competitions, non-recognition by the Irish FA and non-selection for international fixtures. The member clubs accepted these views and on 21 June 1921, the Football League of the Irish Free State was formed in Dublin.

In Belfast, the Irish FA had been caught out by this development. Although it had been aware of the threat of a rival organisation being formed, the Irish FA had not believed that the Leinster FA would pull away from the parent body.

The Leinster FA was not impressed by promises from Belfast that more authority would be vested to itself and the Munster FA, and that more international games would be played in Dublin. The Irish FA was so anxious for the two associations to be reunited that contacts were maintained and when the Football Association informed Belfast of a request from Dublin demanding recognition of the new association, Belfast was concerned that 'nothing should be done that would be detrimental to effect a reconcilation of the new football association with the parent body.'

A conference was staged between representatives of the two associations at the Irish FA's Wellington Place headquarters on 8 March 1924, where the delegates of the Football League of the Irish Free State agreed to give further consideration to a number of the options proposed. These included a suggestion that the international selection committee have equal representation from both bodies with the chairmanship of the body resting with the Irish FA.

After further deliberation back in Dublin, however, the new body asked for the chairmanship of the international selection committee to alternate between the two cities. Failure to agree on this issue led to the break down of the conciliation efforts and the Irish FA carried out its warning to have the new association spurned by the English, Scottish and Welsh Associations. They refused to recognise the transfer of players from southern clubs into their jurisdictions.

Undeterred, the Irish Free State Association sought international acceptance by joining FIFA in 1923.

FIVE

THE DANGEROUS '20S

Belfast Celtic's directors were justified in withdrawing from League football in 1920. The riot during the Glentoran match on St Patrick's Day that year was a forerunner of more violent times to come. In the aftermath of the Great War, thousands of demobbed soldiers had returned to Belfast in search of work and as the fledgling state of Northern Ireland began its life, many of these men found their way into the paramilitary 'B' Specials.

The Ulster Special Constabulary was formed by Sir James Craig to contain the IRA in the North and to pave the way for the partition of the island. The new state would have need of a strong reliable force which was unquestioning in its loyalty. By 1922 there were an estimated 32,000 part-time policemen or 1 in 32 of the population. This force was almost exclusively Protestant and there was no attempt to recruit Catholics, who were perceived to be nationalists and therefore opposed to the existence of Northern Ireland.

'Belfast and Derry were little different from other post-war European cities where there were thousands of war veterans,' explains historian Jonathan Bardon. 'In the Italian cities of Milan, Padua and Rome, fascists and socialists fought against each other. In Berlin and Munich the Freikorps became a law unto themselves.

'There was the fiction going about that, while the Protestants went off to fight on the Western Front, Catholics had stayed behind and had taken their jobs. And of course, they were all seen to be supporters of Sinn Fein and the IRA.'

Unionist politicians played on the fears of the ordinary people by stressing the need to defend the union with the United Kingdom and, at all costs, to oppose an Irish republic. The mass unemployment in the wake of the post-war slump which would rise to 23 per cent by 1922 added to the tension between communities and this was seen as justification for expelling up to 11,000 Catholic workers from the shipyards and engineering factories. It was a volatile mixture which was bound to lead to violence.

This began in June 1920 in Derry before spreading to Belfast, Lisburn, Banbridge and Dromore by July. The Ulster Volunteer Force had re-emerged and sectarian gangs roamed the city looking for victims. On the orders of republican leader Michael Collins, the IRA went on the defensive to protect Catholic areas and to attack the RIC and British Army.

The next two years saw the most sustained period of violence in the city, including modern times, as what became known as the Belfast Pogroms ripped the city apart. Over 450 people were murdered by armed gangs, men in uniforms and snipers. The brutality and intensity of the carnage was best seen in the assassination of women and children. Homes and trams were attacked with bombs and bullets on a regular basis. There was hardly any investigation of the circumstances or any attempt to bring those responsible to justice.

It was estimated that 58 per cent of the victims were from the Catholic community which made up 25 per cent of the population. In the worst months of the violence, between 60 and 70 people were murdered.

In March 1922, the situation reached the depths of depravity with a series of massacres. In the early hours of the morning, a party of unknown uniformed men, believed to have been led by District Inspector J.W. Nixon, broke into the home of a well-known Catholic publican, Owen McMahon, at 3 Kinnaird Terrace, off Belfast's Antrim Road. Five members of the family and an employee who lived with them, were shot dead. District Inspector Nixon had been involved in Lloyd George's reprisal policy in which retaliation was taken against the IRA or prestige targets in the nationalist community.

The following week a raid by the RIC and a group of 'B' Specials ended in what became known as the Arnon Street Massacre during which six people were shot or bludgeoned to death.

Many members of the RIC were Catholics from the south of Ireland who were opposed to the actions of these government-backed paramilitary forces who murdered with impunity. They were properly trained police officers who resented having to work alongside men employed to create terror. Some who may have overheard things became victims themselves as a result of the 'accidental' discharge of weapons in barrack rooms. Others did alert people about possible attacks. Dan McCann, the Belfast Celtic chairman, received a warning and immediately left his shop, got on a tram and escaped from Belfast for a couple of months.

The reprisal policy achieved its aim of spreading fear throughout the nationalist communities and many thousands of refugees headed southwards to safety. Others chose to seek temporary sanctuary at the National Club in Berry Street, and in the seaside resort of Bangor. Joe Devlin condemned the actions of the 'B' Specials in the House of Commons and ironically, when his home at College Square North was threatened with attack, it was guarded by Specials.

The new government of Northern Ireland introduced draconian laws through the Special Powers Act in April 1922, a move that was followed by the internment of 700 nationalists and Sinn Fein supporters. When internment ended in 1924, many of these men, who were teachers and doctors and came from the professional classes, were served with exclusion orders.

These circumstances indicate how difficult it would have been for Belfast Celtic to have competed in football. The Irish League decreased to a membership of five in 1920 following the departure of Celtic, Shelbourne and Bohemians. By the time Celtic returned, the League had risen to 12 clubs.

During Celtic's four-year absence, the people of West Belfast were not entirely without football or indeed a successful club. The winners of the Falls League which was affiliated to the Free State Association were permitted to play in the new association's cup competition. Several of Celtic's players had joined Alton United which won through to the 1923 cup final at Dalymount Park against Shelbourne. When the Alton United team arrived in Dublin, it was provided with an armed guard from the railway station to Dalymount Park and duly surprised everyone present by winning the final 1–0 and taking the Free State Cup back to Belfast.

Meanwhile there was sporting life on offer at Celtic Park where the public had the opportunity to indulge in other sporting past times. Whippet racing, boxing, cycling and athletics, and the

Carnival, came into their own. Some of the atmosphere of those times is captured in these recollections of a Belfast Celtic fan writing under the name of 'Sam Quigg' in a souvenir match programme when a selection of former Belfast Celtic players played against Glasgow Celtic in a charity match at Paradise in 1952.

Those were the days before the introduction of greyhound racing and when on the same afternoon and for a nominal price of admission, one would be provided with such varied sport as whippet racing, pony trotting and boxing. It is impossible to name even a tenth of the men I encountered in the days of the wee doggies, but I remember such excellent slippers as Bunny McCrudden, Happy Dobbin, Jabez Speakman and Billy Dickson.

There wasn't much money about in those days, before the introduction of the Welfare State, and yet there was a fair amount of betting on both whippets and trotting, but the bets were seldom heavy.

Arthur Close was the whippet judge in the days to which I am referring, and he sat in a kind of sentry box. Beside him were half a dozen small flags of similar colours to those of the collars of the dogs and if, for instance, green was the first to flash over the finishing line, Arthur raised the corresponding flag to signify the winner.

Some of the boyos in the early days were up to all kinds of dodges to make their whippets win, or prevent them from doing so. A saucerful of lemonade and a sponge cake were sufficient to stop the swiftest, and at other times I have known the wee animals' toes to be tied with wax end, while rubber bands, inserted under their coloured collars and pulled off at the end of the race simultaneously with the collar, was another way of ensuring that they were not returned as winners.

And what boxing contests we saw in those far off days when men fought for a few quid and provided better entertainment than those of the present day, who get more money for one contest than the old timers received during a lifetime. In the ring on the Donegall Road I watched Davy Magill, Pat McAllister, Johnnie and Billy Maguire,

Jimmy Magee, Hookey Green, Snapper Grant, Jimmy Anderson, Mick Ronan, Jim Dwyer, Pat Breslin, Bobbie Dobbs, the fighting Scot (Johnnie Mathewson) and Fighting Bob Spencer. What memories those names will conjure up to older fight fans!

The Carnival at Celtic Park was to become one of the great attractions in the city and a profitable venture, too. The accounts for the June 1925 venture recorded a net profit of £3,200. In return for the Carnival's success, the board of directors at its August meeting agreed that:

> . . . a sum of £50 was voted to Mr Charles McShane who had done a great deal of work from its inception to its close. The secretary was directed to purchase suitable souvenirs for Mrs E. McSorley and Mrs R. Barr and to Messieurs John Lynch and James Thompson and Hugh McNeil. The sum of £100 was voted to the secretary to mark the appreciation of the directors of the work done in connection with the carnival.

The Celtic Carnival was a huge success. Paradise provided plenty of space for a wide variety of side shows which intermingled with boxing matches, whippet races and athletics. In April 1925, Glasgow Celtic travelled to Belfast to play a team of former Celtic players in an exhibition game in a lead-up to the June event. The Tramways company had been requested to provide an adequate service from the city centre to Paradise. Bob Barr had asked for the provision of 'minute trams'.

When Celtic did eventually come back to football, it was as a result of persuasion and, perhaps, a little bit of subterfuge involving the Irish League's management committee. At the annual meeting of the IFL in May 1923, mention was made that approaches had been made to Belfast Celtic regarding a possible return. And while their directors had stated that the time was not yet opportune, the League hoped that it would be soon. There was an admission that standards had dropped and that the finances were not good. The Irish League needed more clubs. It needed Celtic – and soon.

League president, Thomas Moore (Glentoran), expressed the hope that three clubs from Dublin might return to the fold and that, if they did, Celtic would be sure to return as well.

In Celtic's absence, the Falls League had flourished and on many occasions Paradise had been used to stage matches. The success of junior side, Alton United, in winning the Free State Association's Cup on St Patrick's Day 1923 was a major achievement for that part of the city, but players were restricted in the clubs they could choose to join because the Falls League was affiliated to the southern-based administration. The Falls League's decision to switch its affilation to the Irish FA in May 1923 indicated that west Belfast was prepared to support the local association.

In January 1925, the Irish League was showing signs of frustration at Belfast Celtic's lack of indication regarding its future plans. This reticence had been understandable during the worst days of the civil turmoil, but it was felt that if, in the improving situation, Celtic was not prepared to commit itself to a return, then the Irish League might consider an application from another club which would appeal to the Celtic section of the 'spectatorate'. Extensive work had been done on Shaun's enclosure on the Whiterock Road and a League place might be offered to a club playing out of that ground.

With rumours rife that a new club was being formed to take Celtic's place, a meeting was arranged between Belfast Celtic and an Irish League delegation at the National Club on Wednesday, 6 February 1924.

Ben Madigan, writing in the *Irish News*, held out little hope of any progress. 'Celtic are not enamoured of a return to present-day football, and it would, I am afraid, only raise false hopes to suggest that they will embark on a come-back stunt. Some day, perhaps, but at the moment – No!'

How wrong he was! The following week it emerged that the Celtic board had been encouraged by the talks it had held with the delegation led by John Ferguson. The board's concerns had more to do with the peace of the city than the rebuilding of a team and while it issued an invitation for Ferguson's delegation to come and talk with the members of the Celtic club, it also wrote to the RUC on 18 February 1924 to ask advice on the public order situation (see page 53).

Within two days the City Commissioner's Office had written

back in tones which did not indicate that a rousing welcome awaited Belfast Celtic – even if the letter *was* signed 'Your Obedient Servant' (see letter on page 54).

Nevertheless, the willingness was there on the part of the club and its supporters to return and, six days later, on 26 February 1924, after Celtic's members and board had met with the Irish League delegation at the National Club, a unanimous vote decided on an August return. More than ever, the importance of Belfast Celtic to its followers would be understood. Celtic helped to revitalise a community that had been exhausted by years of violence. Partition of the island had left Catholics within Northern Ireland feeling isolated. The abolition of the proportional representation electoral system would increase that even further. They became a state within a state. They had their own culture, education system, newspaper and, in Belfast, they had their own football team.

In the absence of fair representation, discrimination in employment, and repressive legislation, Celtic was the principal means of interaction between the people of West Belfast and the Unionist population.

As the new season approached, Celtic manager Austin Donnelly set about assembling a side on the field. He upheld the club's philosophy of seeking out only the best players. Their denomination was not an issue. All that Donnelly required of anyone invited to wear the Celtic shirt was that they were of good character and could play football. His first signings were for goalkeeper – his own position when he played for Celtic during the first decade of the century.

Burt Jackson was a Londoner who had won schoolboy international honours and an Irish Cup runners-up medal with Willowfield. James Girvan, the second choice goalkeeper, had experience with Linfield Swifts, Bangor and Willowfield. Alf Bruce and Jimmy McDowell had played in defence with Cliftonville, while half-back Paddy Morris, an ex-Falls League player, had been with Queens Island for one season. Jimmy Kirkwood came from Ligoniel, while Ned Shearman, from Glenbank, could play centre-half or centre-forward. Bob Ferguson, who had moved across from East Belfast club, Dundela, had also played for junior side Trojans. Sammy Moore was signed from Derry. Austin Donnelly pulled a master stroke in persuading

Jackie Mahood first, and then his brother, Stanley, to join from Bangor. Norman Stewart, who had scored two goals for Celtic against Linfield in the 1918 Irish Cup final, also rejoined the Austin Donnelly band wagon, though his business commitments limited his availability to the team.

Off the field, Belfast Celtic secretary, Robert Barr, paid attention to the detail of running a business as he kept the directors informed of all aspects of the plans of the company. On 8 July 1924, when the members were informed at the annual meeting that the club had declared a loss of £103 17s 3d for the financial year, a brief mention was made in the minutes of Celtic's forthcoming re-entry to the game.

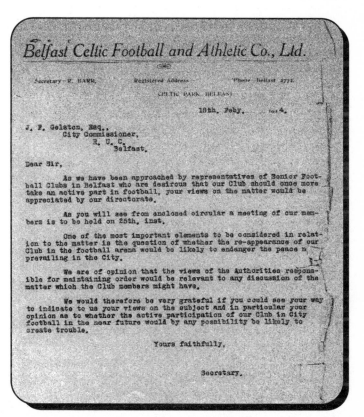

Belfast Celtic Football and Athletic Co., Ltd.

Secretary - R. BARR.   Registered Address -   Phone Belfast 2771.

CELTIC PARK, BELFAST

18th. Feby.   1924.

J. F. Gelston, Esq.,
        City Commissioner,
                R. U. C.,
                        Belfast.

Dear Sir,

        As we have been approached by representatives of Senior Football Clubs in Belfast who are desirous that our Club should once more take an active part in football, your views on the matter would be appreciated by our directorate.

        As you will see from enclosed circular a meeting of our members is to be held on 25th. inst.

        One of the most important elements to be considered in relation to the matter is the question of whether the re-appearance of our Club in the football arena would be likely to endanger the peace n prevailing in the City.

        We are of opinion that the views of the Authorities responsible for maintaining order would be relevant to any discussion of the matter which the Club members might have.

        We would therefore be very grateful if you could see your way to indicate to us your views on the subject and in particular your opinion as to whether the active participation of our Club in City football in the near future would by any possibility be likely to create trouble.

                        Yours faithfully,

                                Secretary.

COMMISSIONER'S OFFICE

ROYAL ULSTER CONSTABULARY

BELFAST,

20th February, 1924.

Robert Barr, Esq.,
Belfast Celtic Football etc Co.Ltd.,
Celtic Park,
Belfast.

Sir,

In reply to your communication of 18th instant.
The question of advising you whether your Club should
re-enter the football arena is hardly one for me.

The danger to the peace of the City is not from
the promoters or teams or the actual playing of the game,
but to possible trouble arising through indiscreet remarks
etc. of even out individuals among the large crowd that
assemble.

If you wish to see me in connection with this
matter at any time I will be pleased to meet you.

Your Obedient Servant,

Commissioner.

'On the general discussion, reference was made by the chairman to the fact that we were returning again to football. He appealed to those present to use their voice and influence towards enlisting support for the team.'

The team trainer, Joe Devlin, who had left Belfast to work in the boxing clubs of New York when Celtic pulled out in 1920, also announced that he would come back. His transatlantic sailing was severly delayed and pre-season training was already well underway by the time he returned to Paradise.

Belfast Celtic's first game was at home to Linfield on Wednesday, 20 August 1924, in a benefit match for the Anti-Prohibition Council. The heavy rain, which had drenched the city all that day, waterlogged the pitch which was in poor condition after four years of staging boxing tournaments. The game was reduced to 80 minutes and Celtic won 2–1.

McGavin put Linfield ahead in the first five minutes. Stanley Mahood equalised 30 seconds after the restart and Jack Mahood scored the winner. The teams for that historic game were:

Celtic: Burt Jackson, Alfie Bruce, Bob Ferguson, Paddy Morris, Jimmy Kirkwood, Jimmy McDowell, Jimmy Gault, Sam Moore, Joe Henderson, Stanley Mahood, Jackie Mahood.
Linfield: McMeekin, Craig, Frame, McIlveen, M. Pyper, Collins, McLean, McGavin, McIlreavy, Cleland, Wilson.
Referee: J.B. Stark.

Three days later, on Saturday, 23 August, the 1924–5 Irish League season kicked off and Celtic's 3–1 win at Glenavon attracted an estimated 4,000 people. Winger Jimmy Gault put Celtic in front after 15 minutes. Weir equalised with a penalty before Stan Mahood scored twice, late in the game.

The Great Northern Railway terminus was packed that day as the team and supporters made off for Lurgan. Bob Barr had advertised for '1,000 mascots' to go to the game. When they all turned up at the station, there weren't enough tickets. GNR could not provide a second train at such short notice and nearly 300 people were left behind. There was bedlam, too, at Mourneview Park where the game had to be delayed by almost ten minutes as the crowd tried to get into the ground. Three of Glenavon's team were caught up in the congestion and the match started without them. The gate receipts of £85 were the biggest of the day. Celtic's return was already starting to pay dividends.

That season the club finished in third place behind Glentoran and Queens Island in the League Championship. And once Celtic had re-established themselves, they were strengthened by the addition of Jimmy Ferris who had been released from England. The inspirational full-back, Bertie Fulton, bolstered up the defence and centre-forward, Sammy Curran, joined the Mahoods in attack.

During the next four seasons Austin Donnelly steered the club to four League titles: the Irish Cup, the Gold Cup, three City Cups and a County Antrim Shield.

The club kept a close eye on its income and expenditure. In March 1926, as Celtic moved towards the collection of all the major trophies, the gate receipts averaged out at £53 per match, while the season ticket holders had paid £232 to date. In previous seasons, warnings had been given to some season ticket holders who were caught presenting their tickets twice at the same game. Indeed some season tickets holders wanted value for money for their investment by insisting that they be given access to the Christmas and Easter sports meetings. The club agreed.

During that first season back in football, Belfast Celtic were drawn against Crusaders in the Irish Cup and the directors, clearly sensitive to any adverse publicity, expressed annoyance towards an, apparently, inaccurate story in the *Belfast Telegraph* which had upset Crusaders.

> A letter was read from Crusaders FC declining an invitation to play an Irish Cup tie at Celtic Park. Attention was directed to a portion of the football notes in the *Evening Telegraph* of the 15th which cast doubts on our playing this match at Crusaders ground. Grave exception was taken to the block type heading of these notes and the secretary was directed to write immediately to the Crusaders club and say that we felt satisfied with their arrangements and remove any doubts about our fulfilling the fixture.

Details of plans to introduce greyhound racing at Celtic Park emerged in December 1926 when the Electric Hare Company, in which Hugh McAlinden had a declared financial interest, proposed to rent the stadium for £500 per annum for periodic meetings. On top of that rental, the secretary of Celtic Park would be paid £100 per annum for duties to be defined later. The acceptance of this offer would necessarily result in the scrapping of the trotting track.

Ten months later, on 28 October 1927, the board was considering a proposed lease to the National Greyhound Racing

Company Ltd, which wanted a 30-year lease at an annual rent of £600. Other conditions included an intermediate payment of £5,000, the equal division of the refreshment room profits and the cancellation of the reservation of the stadium for the month of June.

Each of the Celtic directors was supplied with a draft of the lease proposals in order to make amendments to the various clauses. Mr Fitzpatrick wished for the proposal to be held over for a week, while Mr McCann's objections to the lease were on the grounds that the term of years was too long and consequently the charge of selling the control of Celtic Park for £5,000 might very well be levelled at the directors.

Hugh McAlinden stressed the urgency of an immediate decision and according to the company minutes he argued that:

> with the exception of the Carnival month, we were only leasing what we did not require. Mr McCann agreed that this was so at present, but conditions might be very different long before 30 years had elapsed. Eventually on being appealed to, Mr McCann withdrew his opposition and the motion was passed unanimously.

Belfast Celtic's policy of promoting cycling and athletics was enshrined in its Articles of Association. During the years in exile from football, the staging of these activities had become a central part of the club's commitment to both its members and the local community.

Athletics and cycling were also becoming embroiled in political crises and in 1924 it became apparent that their governing body might fragment in the same way that Irish football's administration had done in 1921. Belfast Celtic was mindful of remaining neutral and the chairman, Hugh McAlinden, and the secretary, declared themselves willing to represent the club at any meeting of the athletic and cycling governing body. Celtic also decided that it would be in its interests not to have any officials from that sporting body working at Celtic Park.

In July 1925, a meeting was held at the Club House, Celtic Park, to form a new athletics governing body for Ulster which would secede from the Dublin-based National Association of Cycling and Athletics.

Representatives from various cycling and athletics clubs including Hibernians, Northern CC, Mid Down CC, Trinity Harriers, King's Moss CC, Irish Road Club, East Antrim, County Antrim Harriers and Moneyrea CC were wholesome in their praise of the way in which Belfast Celtic had strived to promote, and support, both sports.

SIX

INTO THE '30s

When Austin Donnelly stood aside as Belfast Celtic team manager in 1929, he had set an enviable record for his successor. During his two spells in charge from 1915 to 1920 and 1924 to 1929, he oversaw over 130 League games. The team won almost one hundred of these, five League Championships, two Irish Cups, as well as the Gold Cup and the City Cup.

That record would be surpassed, however, with the arrival from Liverpool in 1934, of player–manager Elisha Scott. Several of the intervening years had been comparatively lean as first Archie Heggarty took charge from 1929 to 1932, followed by Jimmy McColl in the next two seasons. Heggarty's legacy was two City Cup trophies, while McColl managed the League title and the City Cup in 1933.

The team that had served Austin Donnelly so well began to break up after those four consecutive League titles between 1926 and 1929, and it would take some time to redevelop a side that would be as consistently effective again.

Mickey Hamill retired to concentrate on scouting and to run his own business on the Falls Road. Jimmy Ferris, too, had to stop playing because of ill health and there were the other usual changes in personnel as Celtic continued its policy of constantly renewing playing staff. Eddie Inch, Chris Fitzmaurice and Stanley Mahood had served the club well and moved on. Paradise was to become the home for a new breed of Celtic stars in the 1930s as Davy 'Boy' Martin, Keiller McCullough, Peter O'Connor, Harry Walker, Jackie Coulter, Norman Kernaghan, Jimmy Turnbull and Jimmy McAlinden became just a few of the names that would play a major role in Celtic's dominance of the decade.

Belfast Celtic's ability to attract a crowd never waned and aside from its commitments to the various League and Cup competitions, it was under constant demand to help out charities and good causes. In January 1932, Robert Barr wrote to Everton football club requesting that it provide the opposition in a benefit game for Celtic winger Jackie Mahood. Such games were common place and an appearance by Everton would certainly have guaranteed large gate receipts.

In part of the letter (see page 60), Barr was clearly hoping for some reciprocity from Goodison Park by reminding Everton of a transfer infringement a few years years earlier. One could certainly not accuse the Celtic secretary of subtlety in his approach

Theo Kelly, temporary secretary at Goodison Park, replied a week later to turn down the request. In his succinct response, there appeared to be more than a hint of favouritism towards Linfield (see letter on page 61).

In keeping with its tradition of giving help where it could, Belfast Celtic constantly granted aid and assistance to what it regarded as worthwhile causes. All requests were vetted by the board of directors.

> The board received a letter from the Mater Hospital asking the club to promote a sports meeting on its behalf. The board decided that the event should be for the joint benefit of both principal hospitals.
>
> A melodeon band asked to play at matches. This was granted though any final decision was delayed until after the band had played at the opening game of the season.
>
> Permission was given for a collection in the ground in aid of the Sports Gala Wireless Fund.
>
> A grant of £25 was made to Mr J. Kearney, the Timekeeper, on the motion of Mr McGinley, seconded by Mr McCluskey.
>
> The Hibernian Harriers applied for and were granted the use of the visitors' pavilion on two nights per week for training purposes.
>
> Sum of £50 [to] be subscribed to the Jim Hanna testimonial.
>
> An application to promote a sports meeting on behalf of the Rev J. J. O'Hara (Banbridge) Church Building fund was received. It was decided to give the proceeds of the

meeting to be held on the 15th to this fund and if necessary to make up the net proceeds to £100.

A letter was read from the Belfast Tramway Board asking for a match against Linfield on March 10th. It was decided to grant the request.

A letter was read from Woodburn FC asking for a grant in consideration of the fact that S. Curran was a player on their team prior to signing for us. Decided to send them £10.

A large number of appeals from various clubs and bodies for financial assistance were read and declined.

Applications for collections and lightning ballots at the next football match were refused owing to the likelihood of such things becoming a nuisance at matches.

The question of bands at matches was left in the hands of the secretary.

Chairman reported that he had met a deputation of club supporters regarding a dance in Hawthorn Hall on 17 March next. He gave the deputation to understand that while he would not like to discourage any useful activities on behalf of the club, the deputation must clearly understand that this function was in no sense official.

The suggested match versus Shamrock Rovers to be played in Dublin on Sunday next was not approved on the grounds that some members of the team had objections to playing a match on Sunday.

Letter received from Ards FC requesting a match on 5 May in aid of a player who had broken a leg. Not a suitable date though the club were sympathetic to the object of the game and if possible would play the match at a later date.

An application for a benefit match for Nazareth Lodge was received. The secretary to reply that it was impossible to find a suitable date.

An application from the Inn Lodge band to play and collect at the Glasgow Celtic match was agreed to.

It was reported that Glasgow Celtic would play us a match in Belfast on Monday, 2nd May in aid of Nazareth House Bazaar Fund.

An application received for a match for the discharged

Belfast Celtic Football & Athletic Co., Ltd.

SECRETARY—R. BARR.   REGISTERED ADDRESS:—   PHONE—BELFAST 2772
                      CELTIC PARK, BELFAST.

———— 19/12/31. ———— 193——

Thos H McIntosh Esq.

  Everton F c.

          Liverpool.

Dear Sir,

        My Club has arranged to give a benefit match to Jack Mahood this season. It has been suggested that Everton might be in a position to furnish the opposition. We are not asking or suggesting that you will travel on easy conditions, but we do urge that you will send your team no matter what the terms are. I ask you personally to remind your Board that some years ago when you had infringed a League rule over signing R.Irvine then on our retain list, we waived all claim and gave his League transfer without conditions or bargaining of any kind. This you will remember was just after your Club had been mercilessly fined by the Football League over some technical breach of regulations.

        Mr Hair of your Board who interviewed us on that occasion will I am sure remember (it was on a Sunday morning and he was accompanied by Mr Smith of the Belfast Telegraph) I made it clear that the transfer was given free and that you were under no financial obligation either immediate or remote but perhaps there would come a time when you might do us a favour.

        Well, we ask one now, not for the Club but for one of its players,

Prisoners Aid Society. The secretary was instructed to reply stating that we would accede if we could and the matter was left in the hands of Mr Donnelly.

Application from Portadown FC to play a friendly at Celtic Park was not entertained.

It was decided on the motion of Mr Fitzpatrick, seconded by Dr McCloskey to give a bonus of £50 to Mr Charles Murphy of the second eleven.

It was decided on the motion of Mr P. McAlinden,

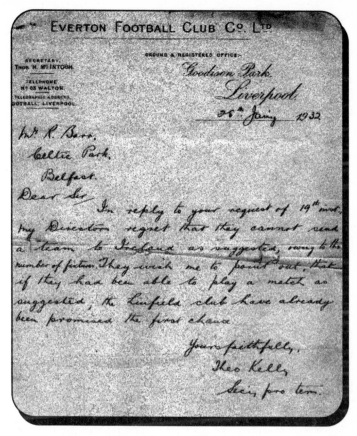

EVERTON FOOTBALL CLUB Cº. Lᵀᴰ

SECRETARY,
THOS H. MᶜINTOSH.

TELEPHONE
Nº 03 WALTON.

TELEGRAPHIC ADDRESS
"FOOTBALL, LIVERPOOL."

GROUND & REGISTERED OFFICE:-

Goodison Park.
Liverpool,
25ᵗʰ Jany 1932

Mr R. Barr,
Celtic Park,
Belfast.

Dear Sir,

In reply to your request of 19ᵗʰ inst.,
my Directors regret that they cannot send
a team to Ireland as suggested, owing to the
number of fixtures. They wish me to point out, that
if they had been able to play a match as
suggested, the Linfield club have already
been promised the first chance.

Yours faithfully,
Theo Kelly
Secy pro tem.

seconded by Dr McSparran to give a pension of 10/- a week
to Ned McGee, a former groundsman who was now old
and in very straitened circumstances.

It was unanimously decided to subscribe ten guineas to
the West Belfast Children's Outing fund.

While Belfast Celtic was prepared to be generous in its support of
worthy causes, the club was always on its guard against those who
would take unfair advantage. Gate receipts from games were supposed
to be split between the clubs involved and there was more than a
suspicion that at many clubs the attendance figures were deliberately

lowered in order to increase the revenue for the home club. The Irish League did appoint a Turnstiles Committee to investigate the problem and in December 1938, it received objections from some clubs about the presence of a Belfast Celtic employee who was monitoring the turnstiles of other clubs, when Celtic were playing at those grounds. Glentoran was vociferous in its complaint about this Celtic tactic and, while the Irish League had to soothe matters, Celtic was unrepentant about its actions: it knew how dependent other football clubs were on the support that Celtic brought with it to away games. The business side of Belfast Celtic was well aware of the ways in which financial returns could be massaged.

Celtic's disenchantment with the format of the Irish League's City Cup came to a head in June 1939 when it informed the Management Committee by letter that it would not be playing in the forthcoming competition. Bob Barr explained his club's attitude and when the committee chairman, George Tate, appealed to Celtic to withdraw the letter and reconsider, Barr agreed to bring the matter back to the directors.

The meeting was adjourned until the beginning of July to allow Celtic more time to consider the matter. At that meeting Celtic could still not give an undertaking that it would compete and, as the League deliberated on extending the deadline, Bob Barr said that he saw no reason why the meeting should be further adjourned.

And with those few officially recorded words, a valuable source of revenue was lost for that year at least.

The arrival of Elisha Scott, Celtic's last manager, saw the beginning of a unique partnership. He had made his name as goalkeeper with Liverpool and would enhance that reputation even further during Belfast Celtic's remaining 15 years in the Irish League.

Scott held the respect of players even though he was tough on discipline and short on praise. In one game, Peter O'Connor scored 11 goals – a record – in the 13–0 defeat of Glenavon. Scott berated him for the chances that had been missed.

He sold players such as Davy Martin and Jackie Brown to Wolves for £7,500, which was a huge fee in 1934. Jimmy McAlinden was transferred to Portsmouth in 1938 for £7,500.

Lish Scott had come up through the school of hard knocks and the single-minded determination which had proved so successful in a long and distinguished career at Anfield continued to be useful in his role as manager.

Scott's achievements at Celtic Park amounted to 31 trophies between 1936 and 1949. As a player he had risen through the ranks of the Boys Brigade and joined Liverpool from Broadway United afer being released by Linfield. His brother, Billy, was Everton's Irish international goalkeeper, but the club felt that, at 17, Elisha was too young to sign.

He made his debut for Liverpool on 1 January 1913 against Newcastle United at St James Park. It transpired that Newcastle had been keen to sign him, but Liverpool manager Tom Watson had rejected the £1,000 bid despite Scott's request on the train to Newcastle to be allowed to leave because of his desire for first team action. Watson's judgement proved to be sound. Scott was to play 467 games for Liverpool.

He stayed on in Merseyside during the early years of the Great War and played in the Lancashire League in 1915–6 before returning to Belfast where he signed for Belfast Celtic. He played in the 1917 Irish Cup final where Glentoran were the 2–0 winners. But that disappointment was set aside a year later when Scott kept a clean sheet in Celtic's 2–0 defeat of Linfield in the final.

Scott continued as goalkeeper at Anfield when the Football League resumed in 1919 and won two first division medals in 1922 and 1923.

'While my father always intended that we should come back to Belfast, we really had a very comfortable life in England,' says Elisha Scott's son, Billy. 'The pay at Liverpool was good, though not comparable with today. Players were given a benefit game every four years and kept the proceeds. That helped to build a nest egg.

'We were living in the middle-class district of New Brighton. Lish had some great friends in the city including Everton's Dixie Deane, but home was always going to be Belfast.'

Scott had kept a house on Belfast's Donegall Road during his time in England. The Scott family would travel back to Ireland when the season ended in May and return to Merseyside in August as pre-season training began.

On 2 May 1934 Elisha Scott said a public farewell to a tearful crowd at Anfield at the end of Liverpool's last home game of the season. While they were sad to see him leave, they were delighted that the public outcry at a proposed £250 transfer to Everton had prevented that move from being completed. Instead, Scott was permitted to return to his native city as player-manager of Belfast Celtic.

Apart from his wife Alice and son Billy, the 40-year-old Elisha Scott also brought back to Belfast many of the football habits he had been taught at Liverpool. He was a lean figure who was very particular about his personal appearance and rarely went out without being dressed in a suit, shirt and tie, clean shoes and a hat. Scott insisted that players appear neat and tidy and were well behaved. At Liverpool the punishment for misbehaviour in public could result in a fine or being dropped from the first team. The same rule applied at Celtic.

Another facet of the Anfield experience, which was incorporated at Belfast Celtic, was stamina training. Celtic, under Scott's guidance, would win many of their games in the last 20 minutes when a tiring opposition would be run into the ground before the final whistle. Slackness at training was noted and the sanctions could be severe.

One of the conditions of the players' contracts stated that in consideration for the weekly wage, the said player:

> shall play in all Club matches when required and shall keep himself sober and in good playing form, and attend regularly to training and generally observe the training instructions, and do all that is deemed necessary to fit himself as an efficient football player.

Scott was by no means a strict teetotaller, nor did he expect his team to be. He did, however, try to impose a strict rule prohibiting players from drinking alcohol on the evening before a game.

'Lish used to have people watching on a Friday night for players going into the bars around the Donegall Road, the Falls Road or Roddy's Bar on the lower Broadway,' says his son Billy. 'My aunts Edith, Elizabeth and Annie were primed off to act as watchers. And he also used touts further along the Falls to keep an eye on the Beehive pub. If he got wind that someone was in a bar, he would go there and stand over them until they went home.'

Scott put great store in the value of money and firmly believed that since players were being paid to play, the public were entitled to maximum effort. One story relates how the manager dealt with Johnny Denver who was having some underpar performances. Scott wrote and posted a letter, purportedly from a Celtic supporter, describing how disappointed he was in the Lurgan player's recent form. When Denver arrived for Tuesday night training, Scott handed him the letter which had arrived, post marked, at Celtic Park that morning. As Denver read the letter, Scott, looking over his shoulder, reinforced the message by saying, 'There, you see. Those supporters agree with what I've been telling you. Remember, they are the ones who pay your wages.'

To this day, arguments rage over Elisha Scott's tactical astuteness. Was he the great tactician who plotted the downfall of opposing teams? Or was he a moderate coach who was fortunate to have the wisdom of players such as Bertie Fulton and Harry Walker?

Walker's memory of the team manager was revealing.

'Elisha was a bit of a martinet and actually his knowledge of football was not great. We used to have a tactical talk on a Thursday night in the boardroom after Lish took the training session. When he finished he would say, "Now we'll decide how we are going to play," and the team would work it out themselves.'

Winger Norman Kernaghan's recollections pointed towards a more co-operative effort in determining the style of play.

'Celtic tried to develop your natural abilities and Lish was part of that club philosophy. When we would have a players' meeting in the boardroom, Lish and the chairman would be there. There would be a discussion on the weaknesses and strengths of various teams, how we would combat these things and how we would cut out their best men. It usually worked. Bertie Fulton, the captain, was a tactical genius.'

Scott was a great believer in road work as part of the fitness programme. In his early years at Belfast Celtic he would accompany the players on long walks and jogs around Shaws Road, Suffolk and Hannahstown.

'When we trained at Celtic Park we used to sprint down one side of the ground and try to outrun the trams going along the Donegall Road,' recalls former player Bobby McAuley.

And ever watchful of players who were slacking in training, Scott used to post people around the perimeter of the pitch during the

Second World War blackouts to make sure that they were running properly and did not take any shortcuts through the gloom.

'Lish once explained his philosophy on the game to me,' says his son Billy. 'His attitude was, you must control your own goal area and don't let the others into it. You must dominate the other area and get the ball in there. Keep the ball moving, don't pussy foot about.'

When the Scott family moved back permanently to Belfast, the worst years of the Depression were having a major impact on the economic and social life of the city. Billy Scott was in his mid-teens and acutely aware of his surroundings.

'I could tell that my parents were very upset by the level of poverty in the city. We were much better off by comparison to most of those who lived around us. There was a shabbiness about them and I can recall the numbers of kids who came to school with little to eat except bread and dripping, and without shoes on their feet.

'There was a lot of disease in the city. TB was rife and I remember whole families being wiped out by it. Young children were dying as well from diphtheria, scarlet fever and other fevers, too.'

Perhaps the scenes of unemployed men hanging round the streets and the starved, pinched-looking faces reminded Elisha Scott of his own childhood and reinforced his reputation for being thrifty.

During his playing days, Scott had limited himself to five cigarettes a day and it is more than probable that the habit, which increased dramatically in later years, was one of the causes of the heart disease that led to his eventual death in 1959. The existence of a cardiac problem was diagnosed in 1934 when he was advised not to play again. Scott ignored the doctors and played on for another couple of years with Celtic and won the last three of his 31 international caps for Ireland.

In his position as full-time manager of Belfast Celtic, Elisha Scott was given a completely free hand in all football matters by the Celtic board of directors. Bob Barr was in charge of the business side of things. Once again Elisha's extensive network of relatives and friends were put to use, looking for new local talent. Scott would sign outsiders, but only if absolutely necessary. 'Give me a good local man who will try harder than an expensive import,' he once declared. This was in keeping with the club policy of bringing young players through the system where they would be ready to slot into place when others were sold on or retired.

On match day, Elisha Scott would never sit on the side line at

Paradise. He preferred to stand and watch the game from a doorway or through a window in the dressing-room.

'Lish could become very highly strung and he had a reputation for having a very rough tongue. Imagine what it was like for the players knowing that he was waiting inside for them,' says Billy Scott. 'I think he was afraid of losing control of himself in public. He was quite friendly with some of the referees and didn't want to get into their bad books.'

Win, lose or draw, Scott rarely seemed to bring any of his footballing problems home with him.

'You wouldn't know from his expression what the result had been. Occasionally he would discuss a game with me and he always discouraged me from following him into goalkeeping. He thought it was too dangerous and he had been unlucky with injuries. He used to say to me, "Never take this up. Never depend on it."'

Elisha Scott valued his privacy. The family home was his hideaway and, while he was happy to talk to members of the football fraternity who called, Lish refused to have a telephone installed in the house. This he felt would be an intrusion which would leave him at the beck and call of others.

'Bertie Fulton and Harry Walker were reasonably close to him and would visit. So would newspaper reporters and friends from other football clubs. They would all be taken into the good room.'

Scott had a circle of football aquaintances with whom he would socialise in Kelly's Cellars. 'Lish could be the life and soul of the party. He loved being in the limelight. He was very proud of his achievements and didn't take kindly to criticism.'

Home was where Elisha could indulge in his great passion for reading. He would buy several newspapers a day and scan them for the world news. If he disagreed with an article he was reading, he would crumple the page and throw it in the fire. Billy would be sent to the library for books on current issues.

'Lish followed politics very closely, but you would never have known what his politics were. He had a great mistrust of politicians. One day he could be a nazi, the next a communist, then pro-Churchill and then pro-Roosevelt,' says Billy. 'He was very anti-war. The family had lost many members during the Great War and when he went back to Liverpool in 1919, he discovered that nearly half the team of 1914 was dead.'

Billy Scott was not at the 1948 Boxing Day game and only heard about the incident when he got home from work. He recalls:

'It was on the radio news and I remember that Lish didn't get home until nearly midnight. He was greatly agitated. I had never seen him being like that before. He couldn't sleep and chain-smoked for weeks afterwards because it upset him so much. Mind you, he should not have been a stranger to a fracas at games between Linfield and Belfast Celtic. The supporters were kept at the two ends of the ground and there was always a big police presence. There would be a gap between the spectators and if trouble broke out, the police would use baton charges to spread them out. The spectators would be knocked down like nine pins, rolling in all directions until the problem was cleared and the factions had separated.

'There was a district inspector called McKenzie who carried a blackthorn stick like a sword. In those days they used to lead their men in the charge. When he retired he gave that stick to my father as a present.'

Belfast Celtic's non-sectarianism policy did not always meet with the approval of its supporters. Scott not only had to endure the taunts of some fellow Protestants, who disapproved of him being in charge of a nationalist club, but also the complaints of Celtic supporters who felt that there should be more Catholics on the team. His response to a supporters club delegation was short and to the point: 'I don't play good Protestants or good Catholics. I just play good players.'

Elisha Scott never gave any view about the club's departure from the Irish League and continued as caretaker manager from 1949 until his death in 1959. He looked after the business correspondence and the upkeep of the ground. It was being used three times a week – Monday, Wednesday and Friday – as a greyhound stadium, though Scott had nothing to do with that.

Glenavon did attempt to sign him in March 1950. The Lurgan side had been without a manager for a year following the resignation of player–manager Archie Livingstone and the Glenavon board of directors saw Scott as the potential saviour of a club struggling to survive.

When Scott laid out his terms for taking the job, the Glenavon board agreed to pay him a salary of £350 per annum and five per cent commission on the subsequent transfer of any player he signed.

Scott also insisted that there would not be any interference in team affairs. Glenavon agreed to that too.

However, the proposed deal fell through when Scott informed Glenavon that he was unable to gain a release from his contract at Celtic Park. The unanswered questions remain. What was happening at Celtic Park that prevented Scott from cutting his ties with a team that was no longer in football? Could it be that the Celtic board was contemplating a return to the game and wanted Scott to remain at the helm? Was the club considering an application to the League of Ireland now that Crusaders had taken its place in the Irish League? Or could it have been a matter of the Celtic board seeking compensation for the terms of Scott's contract and he was not prepared to do that?

Elisha Scott felt that the longer Belfast Celtic were out of the game, the tougher it would be for them to come back. 'As Lish grew older he confided in me that he dreaded the prospect of building up a team again. He felt that he would not be able to cope,' says his son Billy.

Elisha Scott was 67 years old when he died as a result of a series of strokes in May 1959. He is buried in the City Cemetery.

SEVEN

THE WAR YEARS

Following the outbreak of the Second World War, the Irish League Championship ceased at the completion of season 1939–40. In its place a regional Championship was established. The onset of the war would see the return home of many footballers who had been playing in England and Scotland. Among those to come back was Jimmy McAlinden, who had transferred to Portsmouth on 15 December 1938 for a fee of £7,500. McAlinden was subsequently released from his contract to rejoin his beloved Belfast Celtic on the understanding that, when the war was over, he would go back to Portsmouth where he was held in high esteem. In the long chase to sign McAlinden, the Fratton Park outfit had not expected Celtic to be so resolute in its valuation of the player. Despite several visits from Portsmouth manager Jack Tinn and chief scout Jack Foster, Celtic maintained its asking price.

The situation changed when Portsmouth inside-forward, Eden Taylor, suffered a broken collar bone in a game against Stoke and the club needed an immediate replacement. Jack Tinn and Jack Foster travelled to Belfast and agreed to pay the highest ever transfer fee for an Irish player. McAlinden was called to Celtic Park and within minutes had signed for his new club. That evening he was on the Belfast ferry to Heysham. He made his debut against Chelsea a few days later. Before the season ended, he won an FA Cup medal at Wembley where Portsmouth defeated Wolves 4–1 in the 1939 final.

'It was hard leaving Celtic for Portsmouth. But I was realising my ambition to play in the Football League,' recalled McAlinden many years later. 'Jack Tinn was good to me and acted very fairly when the war broke out and I had to return to Belfast.

'It was good to get back to Celtic Park and team up with my former colleagues again. Mind you, not a lot had changed. The discipline was still as strict and you were not allowed to step out of line.

'Once you were a Celtic player that was it. You were not allowed to play in other games, except where it was a charity match and another team had asked permission for you to take part. Lish Scott was very strict about that.'

While McAlinden's return was a joy to Belfast Celtic fans, other clubs, too, were bolstered by the arrival in Northern Ireland of former players and of footballers who had been called up for military service and were taking up postings in Northern Ireland. Glentoran signed Davy 'Boy' Martin from Wolves and Bobby Langton of Blackburn Rovers, while Distillery signings included George Drury, Bert Head, Jack Rowley and Frank Neary. Linfield managed to acquire the services of many guest players and pulled off a major coup by enticing Stoke quartet, Bill Mould, Alex Ormston, Frank Baker and Syd Peppitt, who were serving with the Royal Artillery, to come to Windsor Park.

At Paradise, Elisha Scott would sign two RAF personnel, a young Chelsea centre-half called Ron Greenwood and Brentford striker Len Townsend. Townsend would mark his farewell to Ireland in memorable style: on the eve of his departure, he scored six goals for Belfast Celtic against Derry City, took the boat train to London and scored four goals on his Brentford debut a couple of days later.

On 13 March 1940, the Irish Football League was informed by letter that Harry Cavan, who was to become president of the Irish FA and vice president of FIFA, had been appointed as the new secretary of Ards. At that same meeting, discussions took place regarding proposed wage limits for professional footballers.

It was felt that 'owing to the war emergency conditions', wages should be limited to £1 10s per week and that, where there were midweek games, an additional 10s should be paid. Some delegates suggested that the Irish League should have the power to examine the books of clubs under its jurisdiction and that, where there were breaches, clubs should be fined £25 for each offence.

When these proposals were sent out to the clubs for consideration, Belfast Celtic was one of ten clubs which rejected them.

As Easter 1941 approached, Celtic had all but secured the first Regional League. They were averaging four goals a game and in 20 matches had only conceded 19 goals. Goalkeeper Tommy Breen was out of the side because of injury and Jimmy Twommey was deputising in his place.

A place in the Irish Cup final was assured with a 5–2 win against Glenavon in the semi-final on Saturday, 5 April. Jimmy McAlinden scored twice in the first half, Peter O'Connor added another two and Artie Kelly scored the fifth. That evening at the Oval, Linfield and Distillery played out a 3–3 draw.

The replay of that game was set for the Oval on Wednesday, 9 April, and the game went ahead despite the first bombing raid of the Docks area on the city in the early hours of Tuesday, 8 April 1941.

The Ministry of Public Security announced that 'a small force of enemy bombers, one of which was shot down over the sea and blew up in mid-air, attacked an area in Northern Ireland and caused some damage to industrial, commercial and other property.' The reality, however, was that the destruction was greater than reported. At least thirteen people died as incendiary bombs, magnesium flares, parachute mines and oil bombs landed on houses, timber yards, an aircraft factory and other commercial property on the Shore Road, York Road and the Docks area.

The German Luftwaffe had been testing out the strengths and weaknesses of Belfast's air defences. That skirmish would be replaced by more concentrated attacks in the weeks to come and the people of the city went about their business unaware of the chaos that was about to befall them. In an attempt to improve the protection of Belfast, the government did manage to acquire another searchlight and one anti-aircraft battery.

The Irish Cup semi-final replay between Linfield and Distillery went ahead as scheduled and the Blues won 5–2 to meet Belfast Celtic in the final. Through that week air raid sirens did sound and when the alarm went off during Celtic's League game against Glentoran on Saturday, 12 April, it was ignored by the players and the crowd.

'We were there to play football and we never really thought about there being any danger to us,' said Harry Walker. Celtic won that game with a resounding 8–2 performance at Celtic Park. Peter O'Connor bagged a hat trick, McAlinden scored twice and Norman Kernaghan, Artie Kelly and Bertie Fulton completed the rout.

Legend has it that a German spotter plane circled high above the stadium during that game and that both sets of supporters taunted each other.

It was a busy holiday weekend. On Easter Monday, 14 April, Celtic had four players on duty for the Irish League against the League of Eire at Windsor Park. Although Tommy Breen had been selected along with Billy McMillan, Bertie Fulton, Jackie Vernon and Jimmy McAlinden, he did not make an appearance. A condition of the selection was that he had to have played for Celtic the previous Saturday. Breen had not played in that game against Glentoran and was replaced by Ted Sagar of Portadown for the inter-League fixture. A crowd of at least 15,000 paid £1,609 to hear the band of the Pipes and Drums of the Royal Ulster Rifles and to watch the Irish League win 2–1.

On Easter Tuesday Celtic travelled out of the city to the Brandywell where Artie Kelly scored the only goal in the 1–0 win over Derry City. At Windsor Park and the Oval, Linfield and Glentoran both lost. That evening, at least 90 bombers flew over Belfast again and caused even greater havoc. Bombs, dropping at the rate of two per minute, resulted in the deaths of over 900 people during the five-hour onslaught. As the city tried to identify the dead, and repair essential services, there were reports of profiteers taking advantage of those without homes or food.

'The authorities were keen that life should be seen to continue in as normal a way as possible. And that meant that football should not be disrupted,' recalled Harry Walker.

One Celtic player who was close to the action in Belfast docks was 19-year-old Welshman Tommy Best who had been signed to the club after a spell with Cliftonville. Best was a rating on the Royal Navy minesweeper *HMS Gloman* which had a berth at Pollock Dock, off York Street.

'It was something I'll never forget. There were explosions going off everywhere and we were lucky to survive. Many others lost their lives,' says Best. 'Our ship was unable to go out to sweep for magnetic mines in the Irish Sea for a time because of the damage that was caused.'

Best's sporting ability had been spotted by Sammy Allen, a chief petty officer from Belfast who was also in charge of sports.

'He introduced me to Celtic after I'd played for the Combined Services in a game at Grosvenor Park. I managed to get some first team games on the wing alongside Jimmy McAlinden,' he recalls. 'Norman Kernaghan played on the other wing from me. Those were great days.'

Best has nothing but fond recollections of the season he spent in Belfast. He laughs at the mention of his own place in Irish football history – the first coloured player in the Irish League.

'I suppose it was a bit of a novelty seeing a coloured man playing in green and white. But I can honestly say that I was never subjected to any racist comments from my team mates or any opponents.'

Best was later posted back to England and on to Australia where he continued to play before joining Chester, Cardiff, QPR and Hereford after the war.

After those second bombing raids in the docks area, the disruption in east Belfast was such that it was decided to switch the Irish Cup final on Saturday, 26 April from the Oval to Windsor Park. The kick-off time was also changed from seven o'clock in the evening to three o'clock in the afternoon. Admission prices to the 1941 Irish Cup final were one shilling, two shillings, three shillings and four shillings for a tip-up seat. An estimated crowd of 12,000 saw a Peter O'Connor goal, after 15 minutes, secure Celtic's fifth Irish Cup victory and the trophy was presented to Bertie Fulton by Dr W.F. Hooper, president of the FA of Eire, who had been invited north by the Irish FA.

Linfield's attack that afternoon was lack-lustre against the agile Tommy Breen in the Celtic goal. Marshall had Linfield's best chance to score, but the shot was cleared off the line by McMillan.

The teams were:

Linfield: Redmond, Kirkwood, McNickle, McKeown, Brolly, Wright, Donnelly, Marshall, Sheen, Barket, Baird.

Belfast Celtic: Breen, McMillan, Fulton, Walker, Vernon, Leathem, Kernaghan, Kelly, O'Connor, McAlinden, C. McIlroy.

Two days later, the Cup holders, and O'Connor, were back in action in the Regional League against Cliftonville. The centre-forward's hat- trick in the 3–1 win left Celtic requiring four points from five games to achieve a League and Cup double.

On Friday, 2 May 1941, Celtic travelled to the Oval for a re-arranged League game with Glentoran. The game ended level and Celtic's three goals brought their tally for the season to 99. As the team and supporters left the Oval, they were unaware that this would be the last time Celtic ever played there. Two evenings later, the Oval was devastated in another attack on the city by the German Luftwaffe.

The attack began at 9.45 p.m. and during the following three and a half hours, 96,000 incendiaries and 249 tons of high explosives fire-bombed Belfast. The death toll, which was estimated at 191, would have been higher but for the fact that many people had already evacuated to the countryside. Furthermore, the attack took place on Sunday evening, so there were relatively few people in the city centre.

On Wednesday, 7 May, Celtic secured the title with a 3–0 win at Glenavon.

Peter O'Connor, who had played such a valuable part in Celtic's success that season, also created his own personal place in the history books when he scored 11 goals in Celtic's 13–0 defeat of Glenavon at Mourneview Park. Elisha Scott's belief that centre-forwards were paid to score goals may be a reason why his only acknowledgement of the achievement was to ask O'Connor about the other chances that had been missed.

Scott kept a black book which recorded his team selections and gave performances ratings for each individual Celtic player as well as the match referee. While Peter O'Connor may have created a British record with his eleven goal tally, Scott's assessment was summed up in one word: 'Good'.

On Tuesday, 15 April 1947, Glasgow Celtic came back to Belfast after an absence of 11 years to play Celtic in a friendly game.

The teams were:
Belfast Celtic: Sloan, McMillan, Simpson, Lawler, Ferguson, Wilson, Campbell, McGarry, Jones, Tully, Bonnar.
Glasgow Celtic: Millar, Hogg, Mallen, McPhail, Corbett, Milne, Quinn, McAloon, Kiernan, Evans, Bogal.
Referee: Mr D. Maxwell.

By that stage of the season Belfast Celtic were well on the way to claiming all the major trophies. The visit of the Bhoys warranted a substantial editorial in the match programme.

North Regional League
11th January 1941

A. Celtic v Derry City
T. Breen. Good
L. McMillan. Good
B. Fulton. Good
H. Walker. fair
J. Vernon. Good
J. Leathem. Good
R. Kernaghan. Good
S. McIlroy. fair
P. O'Connor. fair
J. McAlinden. Good
C. McIlroy. Good

Result 4 - 0.
Scorers Kernaghan 1. McAlinden 1.
C. McIlroy 1. Leathem 1.

Referee P. Morris Satisfactory

North Regional League
25th January 1941

H. Celtic v Glenavon
T. Breen. Good
W. McMillan. Good
B. Fulton. Good
H. Walker. Good
J. Vernon. Good
J. Leathem. Good
R. Kernaghan. Good
S. McIlroy. Good
P. O'Connor. Good
J. McAlinden. Good
C. McIlroy. Good

Result 13 - 0.
Scorers P. O'Connor. eleven Goals
an individual club & Irish Record
Leathem 1. C. McIlroy 1.

Referee. W. O'Neill. Satisfactory

It was on 28 April 1936 that we last had the pleasure of a visit from the famous Glasgow Celtic in a benefit match for Bobby Ferguson. It is remarkable that a scan over the teams who did duty on that occasion shows the changes that must be startling to the average football fan.

There are only two players left – one on each side – Bobby Hogg of the Glasgow Celtic and Harry Walker for the locals still carrying the colours of their respective sides and both carrying them with credit and distinction. Of course it must be obvious that there is a fair sprinkling on both sides playing for other Clubs but it must be a bit startling to find that of the teams who took the field ten years ago only one of each lot is on view today.

The teams who took the field in April 1936 were:

Glasgow Celtic – Kennaway, Hogg, Hilley, Wilson, McStay, Geatons, Delaney, Buchan, McCrory, Divers and Murphy.

The Belfast side were – Breen, Fulton, Lavery, O'Connor, Feenan, Scotty Walker, Kernaghan, Harry

Walker, Kelly, Jerry Murray and Matty Geoghan, and the referee was Mr Wm. McLean (Belfast).

Of the teams mentioned, Kennaway returned to his home in Canada at the outbreak of war. Bobby Hogg has already been referred to, Hilley has been out of touch for quite a while, Peter Wilson left to join Dunfermline as manager, Jimmy McStay has since acted as manager of the Club and is at present managing Kilmarnock who now are in the danger zone, Chic Geatons is at present Coach at Parkhead, Jimmy Delaney is at present with Manchester United and on Saturday last was the star turn at Wembley playing for Scotland as centre-forward, Willie Buchan was transferred to Blackpool at a big fee and after service with the Royal Air Force is back again in Blackpool League side, Jimmy McCrory left Parkhead to manage Kilmarnock and, since going there, his side won the Scottish Cup. He will be with the Club tonight. Johnny Divers, inside-left, is now playing with Morton and Frank Murphy, outside-left, is with Limerick.

Of the local side, Tommy Breen is with Shamrock Rovers, Fulton is assisting to run the reserve 11, Tommy Lavery has resigned from football but is still a staunch supporter, Peter O'Connor is acting as general utility man for Coleraine, Johnny Feenan during the war years assisted Shelbourne and is now out of the game, Scotty Walker, a brother of Tommy's, is also out of the game, Norman Kernaghan is at the moment one of the bright lights of Ballymena, Harry Walker has already been referred to, Arty Kelly is with Coleraine after a spell with Barrow, Jerry Murray has just been appointed player-manager of Ballymoney and Matty Geoghan seems to have retired from the game.

Our Glasgow cousins, after a particularly bad start, have managed to secure a respectable position in the League. They are now free from all worries though, of course, they are now out of the Cup. Desmond White who up to a month ago was the Secretary of the Club since the retirement of Willie Maley has now been appointed a director in succession to his father who died recently.

We hope to give the party a real welcome on their arrival in Belfast.

The game against Glasgow Celtic ended in a 4–4 draw and featured Charlie Tully, who would join the Glasgow club the following summer, and Gerry McAloon, who would transfer in the other direction from Parkhead to Paradise.

As Jimmy McCrory, the Glasgow manager, ran his eye over some of the Belfast talent, so too did Manchester United manager Matt Busby, who was a personal friend of Belfast Celtic captain Harry Walker. One player who attracted much attention that day was Belfast Celtic centre-forward Jimmy Jones, scorer of a first-half hat-trick.

Jones, whom Busby would try, and fail, to sign a few years later, was in top form that season and had already notched up more than 40 goals for the club. A bid of £10,000 for Jones from McCrory would be rejected. Four days afterwards, Belfast Celtic sealed the final Regional League title for the third time with goals from Tully and Jones in the 2–1 win at home to Cliftonville.

The following week, Tully was to further enhance his growing reputation with the match-winning goal in the 1–0 Irish Cup final victory over Glentoran. Early in the second half a moment of indecision between Glentoran defenders, Waters and Kane, allowed Tully to latch on to a loose ball. He raced through the open space and drove a left-foot shot past Glentoran goalkeeper, McKee.

In that game Celtic might have had a penalty when McKee was seen to foul Celtic centre-forward Eddie McMorran. However, referee McKitterick judged that the play was elsewhere at the time and took no action.

'It was a disappointment to me when Eddie McMorran was chosen to play that day by Lish Scott,' recalls Jimmy Jones. 'Although I was a very young player, I had been popping in the goals and thought that I might have had a chance to play in the final.'

Jimmy Jones was establishing a great reputation for himself in local football and Elisha Scott's tenacity in wanting the Lurgan teenager to sign for Belfast Celtic would be amply justified.

'To be honest, I never had any intention of signing for a senior club after the dealings I had with Linfield,' explains Jones. 'I'd gone to

Windsor Park as an amateur and was never really given a chance, even though I scored a hat-trick for Linfield Swifts one day. I was used a couple of times as the reserve player which meant I had to be the linesman and after that I never went back. Linfield didn't notice that I had gone.'

Jones continued to play for Shankill Young Men in Lurgan and was eventually enticed to visit Celtic Park when Elisha Scott watched him score six goals in a game.

'I went along to Celtic Park with a friend of mine, Ambrose Wilson, who was a Celtic player and who was in trouble for not reporting back for training. He had been told to bring me along with him.

'Scott took me to his office and showed me all the papers he wanted me to sign. I refused until he opened a drawer and threw me a bundle of 20 crisp, white, five-pound notes.

'I couldn't resist the promise of more money as well, and signed for Celtic. Once I'd done it, I never regretted the decision.'

Linfield did try to rectify their mistake and persuade Jones to change clubs. 'I was at Windsor Park one day and the Linfield secretary Joe Mackey brought me into the office and told me I could name my price,' Jones recalls.

'What really riled me was when Mackey told me that Windsor was my home and that I shouldn't be over there playing with those Taigs [Catholics]. I was happy at Celtic Park. Religion was not an issue. No one cared what you were. I wasn't interested in hearing that kind of sectarian rubbish and I told him to stuff his money and stormed out, slamming the door behind me.

'Mackey never forgave me for that and it would come back to haunt me at the end of that Boxing Day game against Linfield in 1948.'

When the Irish League resumed in August 1947, the power of the Celtic team was reinforced further with a remarkable winning sequence of 31 victories in a row between August 1947 and March 1948. Jimmy Jones was credited with 40 of the 120 goals which Celtic scored during that sequence which stretched over eight months.

One person who did not live to see that achievement was Belfast Celtic's long-serving secretary, Bob Barr, who died in May 1947. Barr, who came from Antrim, had trained as a teacher at St Patrick's

College, Drumcondra in Dublin before taking up a post at Raglan Street School, Belfast, in 1894.

In 1903 he succeeded Alf Lockhart as the company secretary of Belfast Celtic, and worked there for the next 44 years.

Barr's house at St James Park had its own entrance through the back garden into Celtic Park and it seems appropriate that he was close to Paradise when he was taken ill and died at home, aged 72, on Sunday, 11 May 1947. Although in poor health for some years, Bob Barr had worked at the previous day's Inter City Cup game at Paradise where Celtic had defeated Bohemians 5–1.

He was survived by his widow Mary and four sons – Arthur, Edward, Winston and Robert. Winston was named after another brother who had died in childhood, and that Christian name was chosen in honour of Winston Churchill's visit to Celtic Park in 1912.

Barr served one term as Irish League president for the season 1920–1 and did not seek re-nomination.

One of the pivotal players in Celtic's defence during the 1940s was Jack Vernon who joined the club in 1938. His football career had taken him from junior football on the Springfield Road to Dundela and when a trial period at Liverpool, where he was an amateur, did not work out, he returned to Belfast and Celtic Park.

'He loved it at Paradise,' says his brother Charlie. 'He always wanted to play there and jumped at the chance to join the club we all supported. Indeed my brother Harry and I played there as well for a little while, but because we also played Gaelic football which didn't allow people to play soccer as well, we had to use assumed names.'

Jack Vernon won many League and cup honours with Celtic and represented the Irish League, Northern Ireland and the Republic of Ireland before Celtic transferred him to West Bromich Albion in February 1947 for a hefty fee of £9,500. Glasgow Celtic had expressed an interest in signing Vernon in 1946 but felt that he was too slow and overpriced at £8,000. Vernon stayed at West Brom for five seasons before coming back to end his career at Crusaders.

In June 1948, Glasgow Celtic chairman Bob Kelly and manager Jimmy McCrory came to Belfast to sign Charlie Tully for £8,000. The Glasgow club, which had survived the possibility of relegation the previous season, was trying to build a team to challenge Rangers' dominance. Tully was seen as one of the building blocks and his early performances did much to regenerate confidence at Parkhead.

Tully was born on 11 July 1926 at 74 McDonnell Street, off the Falls Road, and his first contact with Belfast Celtic was as a net boy. The club spotted his potential when he was playing schoolboy football with Forth River and Elisha Scott invited him to Celtic Park shortly before his sixteenth birthday in the summer of 1942. In a trial match against a Glentoran select, Tully lined out alongside some of his heroes.

'I was so astounded, shaky and embarrassed that when I got to the dressing-room among such greats as Tommy Breen, Bertie Fulton, Jack Vernon, Jimmy McAlinden and Syd McIlroy, I had to be literally dressed for battle,' wrote Tully in his autobiography *Passed to You*.

'Jack Vernon pulled the green and white jersey over my head and Jimmy McAlinden pushed my first pair of shin guards down my stockings. Before this I had used magazines and newspapers. For once in my life I was speechless!'

Although Celtic lost 3–1, Elisha Scott must have seen enough to convince him of Tully's worth and he was signed the following morning.

'And before my head got the chance to swell, Mr Scott handed me a book of rules. They were as forthright as the man who gave them to me. The book said: "You are a Belfast Celtic player now. No matter who you are, first or second team man, be at the ground at the times scheduled. If you can't read, I'll read it out to you. If you are ill, phone the club doctor or trainer. If the club travels by train or bus, be at the meeting place 30 minutes before hand. And remember, there's only one skipper on the park,"' recalled Tully.

While Scott recognised the impish side of Tully's nature, the manager also had to exert a lot of discipline on the young star who did not relish the rigours of fitness training. As part of his football apprenticeship, Tully was required to clean boots, wash out the dressing-rooms and carry out maintenance duties around the ground.

'Lish was always coming down hard on Charlie,' said club captain Harry Walker. 'Once when he came and told Lish that he had painted the goal posts, Lish growled at him, "Now you know what to aim at on Saturday."'

Charlie Tully, despite his precocious temperament, remained in awe of many of his fellow professionals and admitted that 'times were often tough playing alongside such craftsmen and there were occasions when I didn't think I'd make it. But the coppers were hard to come by and so I stuck with it.'

Charlie spent some time on loan with Cliftonville and Ballyclare Comrades before returning to Paradise. There were concerns about his health when he went into hospital with glandular problems. For a time he used to wear a neckerchief to prevent the abscesses on his neck rubbing against the collar of his jersey. He was back to his best, however, in April 1947 when he played against Glasgow Celtic in a friendly match and weeks later scored the winning goal in the Irish Cup final.

As Belfast bade farewell to Charlie Tully when he left for pre-season training at Parkhead in the summer of 1948, it was noted in the *Irish News* that 'As there is no maximum wage in Scottish football, Charlie should be on big money if he can command a place in the League team.'

In the Irish League, the rate of pay for the semi-professional footballers at Belfast Celtic offered players such as Johnny Denver the opportunity to double their weekly income. As Denver recalls, 'The average wage then was about £4 a week and on top of *that* I was earning about £4 a week at Celtic. Also, I was provided with a season ticket on the train from Lurgan which was about £2 a month.

'There was the occasional bonus, but these were very few. The only time was usually when we were playing Linfield or Glentoran.

'One of the great footballers in England, Stanley Matthews, was getting £12.50 a week for Stoke. Here in the Irish League we were getting about £10 a week, so it wasn't really worth going across to play in the Football League.'

Charlie Tully's arrival in Glasgow was to give the Scottish game a taste of the havoc he had been inflicting in the Irish League. It would also breath new hope into the lives of the Parkhead supporters who had been denied anything to cheer about for a long time.

In September 1948, Tully's individual display in the 3–1 defeat of Rangers in his first Old Firm game prompted the *Glasgow Weekly News* to comment: 'A week ago, at the close of the Celtic–Rangers clash, a crowd of 70,000 – and they weren't all Celtic supporters – lingered behind to applaud the magnificent performance of the smiling Irishman as he walked off the field. Little wonder. His slippery moves, coolness, cuteness, his apparent cheekiness on the ball stamp him as a truly great football craftsman. His very appearance on the field is a signal for a roar from the crowd.'

Belfast barrister, Jim McSparran, was at that game with his father James, a director of Belfast Celtic, and former Glasgow Celtic winger Patsy Gallacher. 'Patsy Gallacher had never seen Tully play before and at the end of that game he turned to my father and said, "James, that is a great player."

'That was praise indeed coming from someone as great as Patsy Gallacher.'

While Tully would play some great games for Glasgow Celtic, including a cup tie against Falkirk at Brockville Park where he scored twice, direct from corner kicks (the first was disallowed and had to be re-taken), his dislike of certain aspects of the game was a source of annoyance for his team mates. Although there was no questioning his football skills, his unwillingness, at times, to help out in defence used to leave the manager in a rage.

Tully's attitude towards training, which Elisha Scott had tried to counter, did not go unnoticed at Parkhead either.

In *'Dreams, and Songs to Sing – A New History of Celtic'* authors Tom Campbell and Pat Woods noted that:

> The charismatic Irishman's aversion to training was demonstrated by his practice of lapping the track only when the club chairman Bob Kelly was watching on his daily visit to Celtic Park. As Bobby Murdoch, then a teenager, has testified, Tully was not above using a combination of blarney and subterfuge to avoid the chores of pre-season training. Charlie timed his arrival at Celtic Park to the second on one occasion when the bus was ready to set off for Ayrshire, where the players would be faced with a ten-mile run to build up stamina. At the last possible moment, Tully rushed up full of apologies – and with a ready-made excuse: he had been unavoidably detained as a police witness to an incident where "someone had fallen off a tram-car". The older hands of the bus assured young Murdoch, about to embark on an ultimately glorious career at the club, that Charlie had probably been peeking around a nearby corner until the bus was pulling out, and then he

would sprint up to the bus, knowing all too well that he no longer had time to get stripped inside Celtic Park without holding everybody up.

Such stories regarding the irrepressible Charlie Tully would have struck a familiar chord with all those who knew him back in Belfast.

EIGHT

THE LAST STRAW

Whitish the Irish League resumed as a 12-team competition in 1947, Belfast Celtic was as potent a force as before and all the signs indicated that its lofty position in Irish football would be maintained. While the editorial in the December 1946 edition of the monthly *Ulster Sports Gazette* was concerning itself with the prospects of a world title fight for local flyweight boxing champion, Rinty Monaghan, an inside-page feature on Belfast Celtic was indicating good times ahead at Paradise. It concluded:

> The present board of directors, with Mr Bob Barr, who has held the office of secretary since 1903 and been a faithful servant at all times, have plans for the erection of a new super-stand to replace the one burned out in 1938. The convenience and comfort of football supporters is the prime aim of the directors, and this, coupled with the provision of a first class team on the playing pitch, should ensure for the future that the Belfast Celtic Football Club will attain even greater heights than ever in the past.

Unknowingly, the club was close to reaching the peak of those great heights and would be gone from the game within another two and a half years. The club concluded the 1946–7 season as Regional League champions and winners of the Irish Cup. At the resumption of the Irish League the following season, Belfast Celtic proved too strong for the challenge of Linfield and, with four points to spare, the Championship returned to Paradise in Spring 1948.

As the new season neared its kick-off, there was little reason to suspect that this would be Belfast Celtic's last. Disputes within FIFA regarding the jurisdiction of the two Irish associations, and a major row at the London Olympic Games, took some of the media attention away from the preparations of the Irish League clubs.

On the eve of the Olympic Games, a serious quarrel erupted when two Belfast swimmers, Edward McCartney and William Jones, were forced to withdraw because they were deemed to be ineligible.

The Irish Amateur Swimming Association, which was an all-Ireland organisation affiliated to the FINA since its foundation in 1894, withdrew the team in protest. The IASA claimed that the International Olympic Committee had changed its entry from Ireland to Eire and that 'according to the rules of the Olympic Games no team can be disqualified or interfered with unless an official objection comes from another country. None has been received.'

The scars of previous battles within Irish sporting organisations seemed to lie behind much of this. The International Athletic Federation made an official statement stating that

> The Eire athletes who were not permitted to compete in the Olympic Games at Wembley today were members of the National Athletic and Cycling Association of Ireland, a body which was suspended by the IAF some years ago. The Irish Olympic Committee were warned of the situation and the IOC asked Eire officials to meet them on two separate occasions but the request was ignored. Only members of the AAU of Eire, as an affiliated body, are recognised by the IAF.

At FIFA's congress in London in July, the Football Association of Ireland had sought support for a ruling that would debar the Irish FA from selecting any players born outside its jurisdiction for international duty. FIFA did not want to interfere with the rules of the British Home Tournament and determined that the Irish FA should continue to select Eire-born men for its home international matches.

However, Congress did reaffirm its ruling that for matches outside the British competition, the Irish FA could only choose players born within its territory.

In October, when Northern Ireland was beaten 6–2 by England at Windsor Park, three of those who played – Jack Vernon (West Brom), Charlie Tully (Glasgow Celtic) and Jimmy McAlinden (Southend) – were former Belfast Celtic players. Bud Aherne was named as reserve.

Soon after that game, Derry Foresters FC withdrew from all competitions under the Irish FA's jurisdiction in protest at remarks allegedly made by Senator W. H. Wilson, president of the North West Football Association. At a Belfast meeting of the National Union of Protestants, Senator Wilson had apparently complained that the selection committee of the Irish FA, containing only one Catholic, had chosen an international team of ten Catholics and only one Protestant.

In its letter to the Irish FA, Derry Foresters FC stated, 'We have always held that religion and politics should not be allowed to enter into the field of sport. The fact that the associations made such remarks calls for a strong protest. We have come to the decision that the most effective protest we can make is to withdraw from all competitions. We have come to this decision in the hope that your Association will take measures to see that no team is again insulted on account of the religion of some of its members.'

By that stage of the season, Celtic were moving into gear. Ten victories and only one defeat in twelve games was championship form and Jimmy Jones was back in the team following an almost miraculous recovery from a serious injury. He suffered a broken lower jaw in the 2–1 victory against Glentoran on 25 August 1948. Fifteen days later he was passed fit to play again and led the attack in the 1–0 defeat of Cliftonville.

'The injury was accidental. I'd been running through the middle and fell. The ball hit me on the back of the head and the defender, who was trying to clear the danger, kicked me on the chin.'

Jones was examined by a dentist and underwent an X-ray at the Mater Hospital. The dentist made a cast for his mouth and tied up his jaw with a big bandage.

'When I got home I took it off because it looked silly. I went back to the dentist again to have a splint put in my mouth. It was meant to stay for three weeks and the only thing I could eat was soup.'

Jones stuck to the liquid diet for a few days before the pain of the splint which was cutting into his gum forced him to remove it. Having filed and polished it, he was unable to open his mouth wide enough to put it back in place. 'I still went down to Celtic Park to train and one evening Dr McSparran came in and asked how it was. I had to pretend that the splint was still there by muttering through my teeth. If he had asked me to open my mouth, I would have been in trouble.'

On 9 September 1948, Jones was put on standby for Celtic's Gold Cup game at Solitude and he underwent a medical check-up at the Mater Hospital.

'The doctor there wanted to know if I was in any pain and I told him that everything seemed okay. He then asked me to bite his finger as hard as I could. It was torturous but I could not say anything. I was then cleared to play again, but I was too scared to head the ball during the game.'

Celtic team captain, Harry Walker, believed that the seeds for the Boxing Day riot at Windsor Park may have been sown when Linfield was beaten 2–1 in a City Cup game at Paradise at the end of October and there was disagreement between Celtic goalkeeper Kevin McAlinden and Linfield centre-forward Billy Simpson.

'There was a bit of a mix up when Billy Simpson kicked Kevin McAlinden as he lay on the ground. I told Billy that Kevin would not allow him to get away with that. The next time the ball came in, Kevin caught it and cleared it, and then hit Simpson on the jaw. The referee didn't see it but most of the crowd did, and I think that caused a rise in tension in the lead up to Boxing Day.'

The tradition of Christmas morning encounters between Belfast Celtic and Linfield had been changed to Boxing Day because of objections. Other clubs were concerned that they were being denied the chance of additional revenue with a holiday meeting against Celtic or Linfield.

Christmas Day 1948 was on a Saturday and Belfast Celtic won 5–0 at Ballymena United. Kevin McAlinden was rested that day because of an injury.

Boxing Day was Monday, 27 December, and Harry Walker and the rest of the team regarded the impending visit to Windsor Park with a mixture of excitement and apprehension.

'Linfield were always our rivals. Out of necessity, the Blues had a good team at that time because Celtic could not be allowed to rule the roost', he recalled. 'It made for great competition. It created interest among spectators and gave Irish football a good name.

People coming across from England saw Irish League football at its best.'

Walker said that rumours going around Belfast suggested that there could be trouble at the forthcoming derby game. Anonymous letters and threats had been sent to Celtic Park warning Kevin McAlinden and Robin Lawler not to play at Windsor Park. The editorial in the Linfield match programme *The Windsor Magazine* welcomed Celtic with the following words:

> What is it that makes a Belfast Celtic and Linfield clash so magnetic an attraction not only to the followers of both clubs, but to many other non-partisans as well? In the past, an 'Old Firm' duel has taken pride of place over every other attraction, and this afternoon the game should be no exception.
>
> The Celts and we have each won one of the two trophies played for to date, and we are both putting up a strong challenge for the Irish League Championship. Prior to the holiday games, we were in front with a three-point lead over the Donegall Road Club, and we can expect them to make a big effort to reduce the leeway. All this adds further interest to our encounter this afternoon, and all we hope for is a grand sporting game and, above all, may the best team win!

In reality, the hopes for 'a grand sporting game' were to be replaced by one of the most shameful episodes of thuggery in the history of the Irish Football League.

Harry Walker recalled that when the Celtic team arrived at the ground, there was a palpable sense of foreboding. 'You could feel it in the air. Before the match I asked Elisha Scott to take Robin Lawler off and put Joe Douglas on. Joe was not afraid of anything. Robin was even trembling before he went out on to the field and I think the match was a nightmare for him until it finished. Some of our team that day were too afraid even to hit the ball.

'I won the toss and decided that we would defend the Railway end in the first half so that Kevin would get away quickly to the pavilion at full-time.'

The game was packed with drama and incident as Linfield, reduced to eight players, struck a late equaliser in the 1–1 draw.

Linfield lost Jackie Russell and Bob Bryson through injury in the first half. Bryson suffered a broken ankle in an accidental clash with Belfast Celtic's centre-forward, Jimmy Jones. A public address announcement at half-time from Linfield's secretary, Joe Mackey, informing the crowd that Bryson had a broken right leg, did little to calm the atmosphere.

Midway into the second half, the dismissal of Albert Currie and Belfast Celtic's Paddy Bonnar by referee Norman Boal added to the palpable tension among the spectators.

Belfast Celtic took the lead with ten minutes remaining when Harry Walker scored from the penalty spot after Johnny Denver was fouled inside the area by Jimmy McCune.

Linfield's competitive spirit was to deny Belfast Celtic a final victory at Windsor Park as Billy Simpson hit an equaliser in the dying minutes.

'The crowd reaction to Billy's goal really worried me,' says former Celtic forward, George Hazlett. 'Even with my background of growing up in a tough area of Glasgow, I had never seen anything like it. When I saw the uniformed policemen, who were supposed to be neutral, throwing their caps in the air with delight, I realised that we were not going to have much protection at the end of the game.'

At the full-time whistle, a section of the home supporters swept on to the pitch for the second time in the game and attacked several of the Belfast Celtic players. Harry Walker, anticipating the trouble, went to McAlinden's assistance. Grabbing one of the iron bars used to secure the goal nets to the ground, Walker used it to try and fend off the mob as the team tried to fight its way to safety.

In the sanctuary of the dressing-rooms where Kevin McAlinden and Bud Aherne had to be treated for injuries inflicted by the rampaging crowd, it was quickly realised that Jimmy Jones was missing.

'Everyone was in the changing room except Jimmy. I never thought of him,' says Johnny Denver. 'They wouldn't let us see him. Joe Devlin, the trainer, said that Jimmy's leg was broken. He was always a player that the crowd liked to shout at. It left other players to get on with the game. Jimmy was a great help that way, but he got the worst of it that day.'

The Celtic players wanted to go back out and rescue their colleague, but were prevented from doing so. At that stage it was too late to save Jones from his fate. When the game ended, he was the furthest of the Belfast Celtic players from the dressing-rooms, but was not expecting any trouble as he tried to leave the field.

'I had just shaken hands with some of the Linfield players when some one hit me on the back of the head. When I turned to see quite a number of people behind me, I ran over to the side of the ground where the police had been during the match but there weren't any there.'

As Jones continued his attempt to escape he was pushed over a wall on to the terracing where one of his pursuers jumped on his leg.

'I didn't realise my leg was broken until I tried to get up and run away but I couldn't. I remember a policeman arriving and saying, "If you don't stop kicking him, I'll use my baton."'

Jones remains convinced that his life was saved by the quick thinking of a friend, Sean McCann, who had been a spectator at the match. McCann, the Ballymena United goalkeeper, on seeing Jones hunted down by a section of the Linfield support, raced to the scene and threw himself over his defenceless and unprotected friend. Even after half a century, Sean McCann, who is retired and living in Belfast, finds it difficult to recall the horrific events of that afternoon.

'I'd had a game that morning for Ballymena and the visit to Windsor Park was not expected to be anything out of the ordinary – until the end, and I saw Jimmy running across to the side of the crowd where I was sitting with another friend Harry O'Neill.

'The next thing I knew was that he was lying on the terracing and, when he tried to get up and run away from those who were chasing him, I realised how dangerous the situation had become.'

McCann leapt out of the stand and down some ten feet into the enclosure where Jones was being attacked.

'It was hot and heavy and there were fist fights as I tried to get to him. No one gave him any protection until I was able to get down close to him. A policeman who was nearby didn't even take out his truncheon. I told him to give it to me and I would use it.'

Sean McCann shielded his friend until medical help came and then he went home. McCann did not appreciate the enormity of what had happened until the next morning when he was asked to go to visit Jones at the hospital.

'When I went in to see Jimmy he threw his arms around me and said, "Sean, you saved my life."'

Jones still contends that the angry assault which raged down on him was due in part to that public address announcement by the Linfield secretary, Joe Mackey.

'Mackey was guilty of inciting the crowd by more or less laying the blame on me for Bob Bryson's injury. I was not responsible.'

Bob Bryson was a journeyman centre-half who had arrived in Ireland from Larkhall, south Glasgow, in 1938 and stayed rather than return to the mining job in Scotland which he hated. He had played at Shamrock Rovers, Newry Town and Glentoran before settling at Windsor Park as a part-time professional with a job at the shipyard. He was completely unaware of what happened at the end of that fateful game against Belfast Celtic because he had already been taken to hospital.

'It was an accidental clash between us. When I went down, I knew my ankle was broken.'

George Hazlett had experience of the frenzy at Old Firm games from his time at Glasgow Celtic, but says it did not compare to the hysteria of that Boxing Day game in Belfast.

'I was the last one with the ball when the whistle sounded. The crowd rushed on like wild animals. I remember Jimmy disappearing among them. There was nothing else for it. It was every man for himself and I had to punch and kick my way to safety.

'When I got to the dressing-room, our trainer Joe Devlin was lying on a stretcher holding his face. I asked, "Did they get you as well?"

"No, it was you," he replied. "I was trying to help you and you turned round and punched me on the mouth." Looking back now it is funny, but at the time it was just mayhem.'

Bob Bryson found out about the crowd attack on Jones the following morning when he was taken to the Musgrave and Clark Clinic to convalesce. Ironically he was given a room next to Jimmy Jones. Both men received visits from colleagues and opponents.

'While there was that rivalry between the clubs, the players from the clubs were good to each other. If you were injured they would come and visit you,' says Bryson. 'Celtic supporters came up to see Jimmy and called in to me as well. I don't know what happened, but I thought the whole incident was terrible and it caused such damage to the image of the game.'

When Jimmy Jones was rescued from the mob, he was taken by

ambulance to the Musgrave and Clark Clinic at the Royal Victoria Hospital where the enormity of what had happened began to sink in. 'The viciousness of the crowd sticks in my mind. It's a thing I've never forgotten.'

Jones faced the very real prospect that his promising football career was at an end, before it had really begun. At the insistence of the club, Jones was treated by the leading Belfast orthopaedic surgeon, Jimmy Withers.

'I would not have played again but for his expertise and skill,' says Jones today. 'On one occasion he came to the Musgrave Clinic to amputate my leg, but changed his mind and decided to wait another few days. Thankfully the leg began to heal, though I still ended up with my right leg shorter than the left.'

The board of directors of Belfast Celtic was furious at what had happened and its anger grew still further with the knowledge that the police had failed to make any arrests. Publicly the board channelled that fury into a statement which was printed the following day by the *Irish News* and *Belfast Telegraph*.

> The attack, the directors feel, in its gravity is without parallel in the annals of football. In the course of it the players were thrown to the ground and kicked. Jimmy Jones, the Celtic centre-forward, received multiple injuries, including a broken leg which may totally incapacitate him from football.
>
> During the whole of this concerted attack, the protection afforded to the unfortunate players may be fairly described as quite inadequate.
>
> In the circumstances, the directors wish to make the strongest possible protest against the conduct of those responsible for the protection of the players in failing to take measures either to prevent the brutal attack or to deal with it with any degree of effectiveness after it developed.

The *Irish News* led its front page report with that statement, while reporter 'Ben Madigan', who was at the game, added his description of the events. He questioned the referee's judgment in not stopping the game sooner when he wrote: 'From the start, before a crowd of about 25,000, there was an atmosphere which suggested that one of the greatest crises in the history of Irish football was likely to develop.' (*Irish News* 28 December 1948.) In his conclusion, 'Ben Madigan' declared that Belfast Celtic had been intimidated into not winning the game and that, 'It was a disgusting sight to watch players after 90 minutes of tiresome play on a heavy pitch, being savagely beaten up by mob elements of Linfield supporters, while police stood by and apparently took all their time to protect themselves.'

In the 28 December edition of the *Belfast Telegraph*, the report of the story included a first-hand account, from the bed-ridden Jones, of what had happened. Jones seemed to be more concerned about the prospect of missing Belfast Celtic's end-of-season tour to North America than the near-death experience of the previous 24 hours.

But the article did conclude that: 'Scenes such as Monday's are unparalled in the history of Irish soccer. There have been rows amongst spectators frequently, but never a mass attack. The small force of police were helpless against the mob.'

Belfast journalist James Kelly had been in the main stand on the day of that game and he witnessed genuine shock among spectators at the savagery of the attack. He described the scene as being so overpowering that he thought it was the end of football at that time.

> It was horrifying when the crowd invaded the pitch at the end of the game. The other players seemed to get through, but Jones ran around like a deer with these others after him. This so-called respectable man in a rain coat rushed forward and started kicking him. The police were standing around but they didn't do anything.
>
> Some of the Linfield ticket holders were disgusted by it. I remember one particular man, a well known solicitor, going along the back of the stand where there was a corridor leading to the Linfield rooms. He was so incensed, he was shouting, 'This is what I think of your bloody team,' and he threw his membership card at the door.

The Linfield board of directors held its own meeting to examine the repercussions of the Boxing Day riot and issued a statement which attempted to distance the club from the behaviour of an element of its support.

The Committee, at a special meeting, had under consideration the events which took place at the conclusion of the Boxing Day match. In addition to expressing their strongest disapproval of the unsportsmanlike conduct of a comparatively small section of spectators who rushed the playing pitch and attacked a few of the Celtic players, they especially deplore the attack on Jimmy Jones, the Celtic centre-forward.

The Committee desire to tender sincere sympathy to Jones and express their deep regret at the injuries he has suffered, and desire to assure him that, not only do they deprecate such ungentlemanly conduct, but they are determined to take all possible steps to stamp it out, and with that end in view, they are arranging a conference of all the appropriate authorities.

The Committee believe that a number of spectators may have felt incensed by the serious injury to Bob Bryson, the Linfield centre-half, in which Jones was involved, but they are satisfied that this was a pure accident, for which Jones could not be held responsible. But in any event, no accident or occurrence on the field of play could justify conduct so alien to the high Linfield tradition.

The Committee trust that all those injured, on or off the field of play, will enjoy an early and complete recovery, and that such a demonstration of downright rowdiness will never again be witnessed at any Association game.

For their part, the Committee are determined to leave no stone unturned to punish the perpetrators, and to take effective steps to prevent a recurrence of such regrettable scenes. The Committee feel that, in expressing their views, they have voiced not only the sentiments of the Linfield members, but also those of the great majority of the devoted Linfield following, whose great appreciation of the magnificent outcome of the match was completely overshadowed by the deplorable aftermath, precipitated by the ungallant and unsporting conduct of those who had no official connection with the club.

As the public digested the gravity of the incidents, the Irish FA

Protest and Appeals Committee met for two hours behind closed doors on Tuesday, 4 January 1949 to consider referee Norman Boal's report. The committee said it took a 'serious view of the incident' and decided to punish Linfield by closing its ground for a month – up to and including 1 February.

The *Irish News* reported:

> The Linfield Club will lose two home games as a result: (1) against Ballymena United on 15 January and (2) against Glentoran in the Irish Cup on 22 January. The club has arranged a switching of fixtures with Ballymena so that the match on 15 January becomes an away match (at Ballymena) for Linfield, and the return on 22 April which was fixed for Ballymena will be at Windsor Park.

Within the Irish FA, the representatives of some clubs expressed reservations about the way the issue had been handled. In particular, Mr Kennedy, Ballymena United's representative on the Emergency Committee, pointed out at the 11 January meeting that his club had never agreed to Linfield reversing its home fixture in order to play at Ballymena on 15 January, despite evidence that 'Linfield had stated this in a letter to the Irish League'. Another delegate, Mr McClatchey, was unhappy that the Senior Clubs Committee had not laid down any ruling or attempted to take any step to prevent the singing of party songs at grounds.

Linfield continued to defend its reputation by announcing that it had been trying for two years to erect a perimeter fence around the pitch, but was not able to do so because of steel shortages in post-war Britain. The Amalgamated Blue Supporters Club also expressed its concern at the events at the Boxing Day game and on 6 January 1949, secretary William McKechnie wrote to Belfast Celtic expressing apologies for what had happened (see opposite page).

The issue of the inadequate policing of the Linfield–Belfast Celtic game was raised in the Northern Ireland Parliament at Stormont where the accusations and counter claims fell into the predictable lines. Linfield chairman Harry Midgley, who was a Unionist MP, denied claims that he was guilty of inciting players by the singing of sectarian songs at private gatherings in certain sports clubs. In the

AMALGAMATED BLUE SUPPORTERS' CLUB.
ADVISORY COMMITTEE.

Hon. Secretary :
Mr William McKechzie,
14 Mountcollyer Road,
Belfast.

Meets first Tuesday each month.

Date................6/1........1949

Dear Sir

At the monthly meeting of the above committee I was instructed to write to you regarding what happened at Windsor Park on 27th Dec 1949. I would have wrote to you sooner but I wanted to contact the different clubs of the Amalgamated of which we have 34 clubs. I have been assured by these clubs that not one of them had anything to do with what happened and are deeply concerned at what happened and through you extend our deepest sympathy to all Players and hoping J Jones will have a speedy recovery.

I am Dear Sir
Yours Truly
Wm McKechnie Hon Sec

law courts, Jimmy Jones launched a £10,000 malicious injury claim against Belfast Corporation.

The letters page in the *Irish News* attracted a huge reaction from the public as continual updates on the health of Jimmy Jones were printed.

One reader, signing himself 'An English Doctor' expressed a visitor's sentiments on the events at Windsor Park. He concluded that Belfast must 'contain some of the most barbarous citizens possible. In seven years' war experience I searched my brain for a parallel to Monday's conduct and could find none.'

The reader questioned how this could happen in broad daylight under the noses of the police who seemed to be helpless and confused, and suggested that 'a couple of good English policemen would have cleared the pitch in five minutes and prevented this uncontrolled cannibalism.'

A Belfast Celtic fan suggested that Linfield were not without blame and that they had made no effort to protect the Celtic players. The 'much vaunted efficiency of the RUC' was also queried and there was a recommendation as to what the Celtic delegate to the IFA should demand at its next meeting: 'the protection of the Windsor Park playing pitch by spiked railings, so that the scenes which disgrace the name of Northern Ireland in the sporting world are not allowed to occur again'. The reader also proposed the appointment of cross-Channel referees at these big games and lastly, and very tellingly, 'if the Celtic demands are not met, Celtic should withdraw from football altogether as they did some years ago.'

In another letter, the complainant pointed out that the outrage would be attributed to 'irresponsibles', but that this would hide a multitude of actions which have the support of some very responsible elements 'not only in sport but in other features of Belfast life'.

The writer asked this question of the 'responsible' Linfield sporting following, presuming that they were in the majority – 'What did they do to restrain the hooligan element? Did they make any effort to protect or help the Celtic players? What treatment did Jones receive when he reached the reserved area?'

The reader also stressed that the RUC, 'our police, our *armed* police, whose praises are so well sung by the Home Minister, could not afford any protection to the unfortunate eleven players'. The letter indicated that 'the threat of drawn revolvers could have saved the situation.

'It will take more than "irresponsibility" arguments to explain away Monday's outrage. Drastic diseases need drastic remedies. There is one drastic course open to Celtic as a team with sporting character and a sense of honour and dignity and I sincerely hope they will take that course and pursue it until the Belfast football enthusiast learns the meaning of the word sport.'

One Linfield supporter wrote to the *Irish News* expressing sympathy with the Celtic players. The fan accused the RUC of being ineffective in not drawing their batons to deal with the mob. 'I personally think that all supporters' clubs should be immediately disbanded as these clubs are encouraging mob law.'

A reader who signed off as 'Seven Towers' wrote:

> As the fair name of football has been so wantonly dragged in the mire by a mob of hooligans it is the duty of all true sportsmen to demand in the best interests of the game that responsibility for this outrage should be squarely placed on the shoulders of those either actively or passively responsible.
>
> The Linfield team cannot under the circumstances even claim the moral victory which the eight-man handicap would perhaps suggest.
>
> The club officials would also do well to realise that sport should not be prostituted by religion or politics.
>
> It is a poor commentary on football in Northern Ireland to say that Celtic with their undoubted superiority in numbers and skill dared not win this game.

One could be forgiven for thinking that the following correspondence might have been received from a member of the Celtic board who was testing out public reaction to any suggestions that the club should withdraw from the Irish League.

> Sir – In your report of the attack by Linfield 'sportsmen' on the Celtic team, it is suggested that the affair may lead to 'repercussions in League football.' Quite rightly so. And the one repercussion it should lead to is the immediate withdrawal of Celtic from all competitions governed by the home bodies and a request for entry into the League. In these days of quick air travel this could easily be arranged and would at once leave Irish football flat. Then look at the victories Linfield would have! Look at the gates, too!
>
> This would be much preferable to present conditions, under which both Celtic players and spectators take their lives in their hands when attending a match in either capacity. The affair may have surprised any visitor to Belfast who was present, but not anyone who is familiar with the state of affairs here.

The letter concludes:

> The various Celtic supporters' clubs should call a monster meeting and demand a withdrawal as mentioned above. As to the players, personally, if I were a Celtic player, nothing on earth would induce me to enter Windsor Park again after Monday's display.

> Yours etc., FAIR PLAY

At Paradise, the Belfast Celtic board met in private to consider the club's future. Although little information was emerging from the boardroom, the official programme editorial for the home game against Distillery on Saturday, 8 January 1949 gave some indication of what the directors were thinking.

> Recent events have put a damper on soccer games in the North, and we hope we will be excused if we make no further mention of them than to say they are by no means forgotten. Jimmy Jones is progressing very slowly. It must be very irksome for a young lad full of vigour to lie in one position for almost six weeks. Kevin McAlinden is still on the injured list.

The editorial welcomed Distillery to the Park, referred rather pointedly to the previous week's game – the first since the Linfield game – and then proceeded to question the overall standard of refereeing in the Irish League.

> Our game against Glenavon Saturday last, with a number of team changes owing to injuries, saw us keep on our winning ways. The match was very enjoyable, and even if we won pulling up, it did not detract in any way from the strenuous game put up by the Lurgan men.
>
> We have again to harp on the scarcity of good referees this season. We have some capable referees, even men capable of taking charge of International matches, but we are of the opinion that in some matches on this side, cross-Channel referees should be invited to officiate.

Perhaps though, the Belfast Celtic board was already laying the plans for withdrawal from the Irish League and the club was never expecting to benefit from any improvement in the standard of the referees.

Jimmy Jones recalls that as he lay recuperating in hospital, he overheard a remark which would, in hindsight, prove to be very significant.

'The night that I had my leg broken, Dr McSparran and his son came to see me at the Musgrave Clinic. There had been a meeting of the directors that night and I remember him saying, "This is us finished with Linfield and Irish League football." Whether this was the main reason for Celtic leaving football I don't know.

'Maybe there were others things and when everything was added together, this was a contributory factor. I think the Boxing Day fiasco at Windsor Park was what pushed them over the precipice.'

As Northern Ireland settled into the new year, life continued on and off the field, and in the corridors of power.

Jimmy Jones left the Musgrave Clinic on Friday, 11 February and went home to Lurgan to recuperate. The *Irish News* reported that he would be unable to play football again for at least a season, but was 'likely to make the trip to America in deference to the flood of letters arriving at Celtic Park from the USA'.

It took more than a year for Jones to recover and on medical advice he was unable to travel to America with Celtic. Although the serious leg injury left him with a permanent limp, Jones did make a return to football in 1950 with Larne and then Fulham. However, there were problems regarding his registration at Craven Cottage and he came back to continue his goal-scoring exploits with his home town club, Glenavon. He won three international caps for Northern Ireland in 1956–7.

In the subsequent court case, malicious injury claim against Belfast Corporation – Judge Bernard Fox, sitting at Belfast Recorder Court, found in favour of Jones. An award of £4,361 compensation was made to cover loss of earnings and a share of any possible transfer fee, pain and suffering caused, and medical bills and expenses.

In his judgement, Judge Fox said:

> I have no doubt in concluding that Jones was forced
> or hustled over the parapet by a hostile crowd; that

the fall did not cause the injury to his leg; that the injury was caused by a violent kick after he had got up and started to run; and that he was kicked by members of the crowd consisting of about twenty persons who had followed him over the parapet and who were actuated by ill will towards him.

In the aftermath of the Boxing Day riot, the IFA Senior Clubs Committee suspended Albert Currie until 20 May, while Paddy Bonnar, still protesting his innocence at having verbally abused one of the linesmen, was given an eight-week suspension. Belfast Celtic's sense of injustice can only have been further increased by an Irish FA decision on Friday, 10 March to reduce Currie's suspension to 31 March and fine him £10. There were objections on the basis that Currie's application for reconsideration of the sentence should not have been discussed because it was not on the agenda of the meeting.

Two days before that suspension was due to be completed, the IFA refused to approve that decision of the Senior Clubs Committee, and Albert Currie's original punishment was reinstated.

During March 1949, Celtic announced details of its intended ten-game tour to America. The itinerary would open with a match in New York on 2 May at Triborough Stadium, Randall's Island.

That same month, Belfast Celtic began the disposition of its more valuable assets. Johnny Campbell and Robin Lawler joined Fulham for an 'undisclosed, but record fee'. Fulham's manager Frank Osborne travelled to Belfast to get their signatures on Wednesday, 9 March 1949. The agreement included a clause which would permit them to travel to America, though both players had to withdraw from the Irish League team to play the League of Ireland on St Patrick's Day. Six days later, Tom Aherne had also left Celtic. He signed for Luton Town.

In Harry Walker's opinion those transfers confirmed his suspicions about Celtic's future. 'I had an inkling the club was going to leave football, the day after Johnny and Robin were transferred. When I arrived for training, the first person I saw was Frank Osborne. "What are you doing here?" I asked.

"I want you to come to London."

"You must be joking. I'm 37 years of age."

"Really. I only want you to play for two years and then I'll make you assistant manager."

"It's interesting Frank, but what do Celtic say?"

"I've spoken to them and they want £3,000."

"£3,000 for a 37-year-old! I'll tell you what, Frank. If I get the £3,000 I'll go. If I don't, I won't go."

'Celtic wouldn't agree to me getting £3,000 so I didn't go. But I realised then that the club was doomed to disappear.'

On the more immediate horizon was the impending return league fixture with Linfield, at Paradise, at the beginning of April. Celtic wrote to the Irish League reminding it of what had occurred in the Boxing Day match and, mindful of any potential threat to the peace of the city, the club asked the Irish League to consider cancelling or postponing the game.

Celtic's representatives, Dr McSorley and Dr McSparran, dissented from the decision that a deputation from the Irish League and the two clubs should meet the RUC to discuss the matter.

The game did go ahead and, in a subdued atmosphere, Linfield were 1–0 winners. By the time the Irish League's management committee met again on 29 April to record that the game had been played without incident, and to read out a letter of resignation from Belfast Celtic, the news was already known and Celtic had sailed for America. It may have been that the Celtic board did not want any great outcry at its decision to withdraw membership and was trying to minimise public reaction.

As the *Irish News* was reporting that in New York advance ticket sales for Celtic's forthcoming tour were the highest ever recorded for an overseas soccer team, the story beneath that was significantly more important.

> It has been authoritatively learned that the Irish Football League has received a letter from Belfast Celtic Club requesting permission to withdraw their membership.
>
> No other information is likely to be available until the team and their officials return from their American tour.

On Sunday, 25 April, the *Scottish Sunday Sport* questioned how such a big club could, in the space of a couple of weeks, be allowed to sell its best players and then withdraw from the Irish League.

Can you imagine such a situation in Scottish Football? Belfast Celtic are just as big shots in Ireland as the Rangers are over here.

What would happen, I wonder, if Mr Struth and his directors cashed in on George Young, Ian McCall, Willie Woodburn, Willie Waddell, Willie Thornton and all the rest of them and then quietly sent a note to the Scottish League saying they had decided to withdraw from the competition?

It was almost as if the affair was being stage-managed by Celtic. Perhaps its determination to leave football was so strong that the last thing it desired was an uprising of public support similar to that in 1920 which had briefly drawn it back from the brink.

NINE

AMERICAN FAREWELL

In June 1948, Liverpool and Djurgarden, Stockholm, became the first foreign teams to be permitted to play each other on American soil. The success of that venture had been such that an international series to include teams from Europe and America was organised for the following May and June by the United States Soccer Football Association and the American Soccer League. These bodies had arranged five 'dream games' to be played at Triborough Stadium, Randall's Island: Ireland v the USA, Ireland v Scotland, Sweden v Ireland, England v Sweden and Scotland v the USA.

An invitation was extended to Belfast Celtic to be Ireland's representatives and it sought permission from the Irish FA to compete.

> On the motion of Mr Magill, seconded by Mr Beggs, permission was unanimously granted. The President (Mr F. J. Cochrane) expressed to the Celtic Club good wishes for a happy trip and felt that the invitation was a distinct honour for a club in our Association to receive. Mr Donnelly, on behalf of Belfast Celtic FC, thanked the President for his kind remarks.

Celtic completed its Irish League programme with a 4–3 win over Cliftonville on Thursday, 21 April 1949 and, six days later, the official party set sail for America from Cobh, County Cork, on the 35,000-ton cruise liner the *Mauretania*. The players who travelled were Tom Aherne, Paddy Bonnar, Johnny Campbell, Charlie Currie, Johnny Denver, Joe Douglas, Tom Dorman, George Hazlett, Robin Lawler, Billy McMillen, Kevin McAlinden, Alex Moore, James

Murdough, Mick O'Flanagan, Reggie Simpson and Harry Walker. They were accompanied by Elisha Scott, trainer Paddy McGuigan, chairman Austin Donnelly and directors Dr James McSparran and Patrick McAlinden. The injured Jimmy Jones had hoped to accompany the party, but his doctor refused to allow him to travel.

'We really enjoyed the crossing, it was a great adventure,' recalls Alex Moore, the Glenavon centre-forward, who replaced Jones on the American tour. 'I was invited to go along about six weeks before the trip. It was a great honour and I kept a record of it all in a diary. On the *Mauretania* we kept in shape by training in the gym every day and playing five-a-side games on the deck. Other passengers used to gather round and watch.'

The ship's arrival was delayed by a day due to fog and when it docked in New York on the morning of Tuesday, 3 May, the publicity machine was well underway in promoting interest in the tournament.

Erwin Single wrote in the *World's Sports Extra*:

> The main attraction on 22 May will be the first American appearances of the Scottish International Team, currently conceded to be the 'best soccer team in the world'. A cable from Scotland at the weekend confirms the fact that the self-same team that defeated England by 3–1 and set off a greater victory celebration than V.E. Day will be the one to tour the United States.

Single pointed out that five of the Scottish party were from the 'famed Glasgow Rangers' and that they would be 'tackling Belfast Celtics on the Sunday of Decoration Day weekend'.

The highlight of the series was to be a doubleheader at Triborough Stadium featuring Newcastle United against Kamraterna, Gotenborg, followed by Scotland against the United States. The organisers, who included USA internationals James McGuire and Erno Schwarcz, felt that this would be ideal preparation for the USA squad. It was attempting to qualify for the 1950 World Cup finals in Brazil through the North American Zone finals in Mexico that September.

Of Belfast Celtic's preparations for the tournament, Erwin Single wrote:

By plunking over a stiff insurance guarantee, they have secured three of their brightest stars back from Fulham of the English League. Not content with this acquisition, they have also signed on Chappie Moore of Glenavon, the leading scorer in the Irish League, and three other forwards from rival Irish clubs.

When Belfast Celtic had transferred Robin Lawler and Johnny Campbell to Fulham, Tom Aherne to Luton Town and Paddy Bonnar to Barnsley, the club had secured the releases of those players for the American tour. Alex Moore of Glenavon, John Murdough of Crusaders, Tom Dorman from Ards and Bohemians amateur, Mick O'Flanagan, were the additional players to the squad.

Scotland would have reason to remember the names of Campbell and Moore when Belfast Celtic played them on Sunday, 29 May 1949.

Once the Belfast Celtic party had settled into its New York base at the Paramount Hotel, West 46th Street, the team's first function was an official visit to City Hall to meet Mayor William O'Dwyer. Then it was down to training and preparation for the opening game on Sunday, 8 May at Randall's Island against the New York All-Stars – a select team from the Brookhatton, Hispano and Hakoah clubs.

Any lack of match practice was not immediately apparent as Belfast Celtic established a 2–0 half-time lead. Paddy Bonnar scored a penalty after George Barr handled in the 42nd minute and Johnny Denver added the second with a 25-yard volley, fired past goalkeeper Gene Olaf, a minute before the interval.

The home side, made up of players representing 11 different nationalities, was transformed in the second half. Cuban exile Jesus 'Pito' Villanon pulled a goal back within ten minutes of the restart and, as Belfast Celtic visibly began to tire, Armenian Yeprem Chacurian headed in the equaliser after 69 minutes.

In the words of Erwin Single:

> By game's end, it was Belfast, not New York, that did the puffing. While the Celtics had not exactly disappointed, the fans just weren't prepared to see a picked team from three local clubs dish up so aggressive a brand of soccer. American soccer has

come a long way these past three years and proof of
the pudding was this moral victory by the hobbyists
over the specialists.

The 15,000 crowd got more football than it had been expecting.
There was a preliminary game at which New York Americans drew
2–2 with the Philadelphia Nationals for the American Soccer League
Championship. The championship had to be settled following the
end of the main game, when these two teams re-took the field and
played five periods of extra time – 49 minutes in all. The Nationals
eventually claimed the title when American defender Bibi Ossowsky
needlessly conceded a corner kick.

Belfast Celtic was glad to shake off the effects of the long sea
journey from Ireland and get that opening game completed. Next
day in the *Brooklyn Eagle*, sports writer Leo Kieran analysed what he
had seen. While agreeing that the standard and popularity of soccer
in America was rising, Kieran argued that if some kind of rule
change was made to produce a winning score, the sport would
become more attractive.

> Once in 1939, the New Yorkers tied a team of Scots, but
> lost in overtime play-off. Yesterday, however, there was no
> overtime play, the play having been arranged under
> European rules in which no overtime is permitted.
>
> The fact that the contest drew a 15,000 gate at $2.50
> top was proof that the popularity of the game here as a
> spectator sport is on the rise.

Leo Kieran supported the views put forward by some spectators that
the offside rule should be removed, that substitutions should be
allowed and that time wasting should be penalised.

Elisha Scott would have been interested to read those
observations though his thoughts may have been more on the news
reports which would have been wired back to Belfast. In the parade
around the baseball stadium before the game, Scott was asked,
without any warning, to help Charles Connolly, editor of the *Irish
Echo*, carry a huge tricolour flag. That incident was to create a
political outcry from some of the more extreme elements back home
in Northern Ireland.

Belfast Celtic's second game of the North American tour took the club to Toronto on 11 May, where it had a few days to prepare for the Saturday evening game against Ulster United. During the team's stay at the King Edward Hotel, Elisha Scott imposed a 10.30 p.m. curfew on his players.

'The boys are here for a good time, but they are also here to display their wares at soccer and if we let them run loose their play will suffer,' explained chairman Austin Donnelly, when the local media covered a Celtic training session at the city's Riverdale Park.

The holiday experience did not affect the visitors too much: the challenge from Ulster United at the Maple Leaf Stadium never materialised as Celtic cruised to a 5–0 victory with goals from Hazlett (two), Dorman, O'Flanagan and Campbell. Hazlett was forced to miss the next two games because of a twisted ankle.

Celtic flew back to New York for a game the following day against the Kearny Jersey All-Stars, in front of a crowd of 8,500, at the grounds of Kearny High School. Johnny Campbell broke the deadlock late in the first half with Tom Dorman and Alex Moore adding to the eventual 3–0 tally in the second half.

The tourists managed a few days' rest before they were on the move again to Fall River, Massachusetts for an evening game with the New England All-Stars on 18 May. Fall River's pedigree as a football town had been established in the early years of the century by immigrants who had settled there to work in the cotton mills. After the Second World War, the game was revitalised by the Portuguese community. Any thoughts that this would be an easy game were dispelled early on as a very skilful New Englanders team brought Celtic its first defeat. New England scored twice inside four minutes of the first half to leave Celtic reeling from the power and accuracy of its passing.

John Millington put the home side ahead after 22 minutes following a handball infringement on the edge of the area. His free kick ricocheted off the Celtic defensive wall and beyond the reach of Kevin McAlinden. Centre-forward Mackie Almeida made sure the ball was in the net, but the referee Charley Carvalho had already signalled the score and credited it to the left-winger. Frank (Shorty) Moniz created the opening for Almeida to score the second in the 26th minute. His cross-field pass from the right-wing went into the path of the centre-forward who out-sprinted Billy McMillan to the ball and lobbed it beyond the reach of McAlinden.

The New England All-Stars had chances to increase the score further, but these were wasted by Millington and John Souza.

Celtic's superior fitness began to show in the second half as the New England goal mouth came under constant attack. Goalkeeper Walt Romanowicz made several important saves before Harry Walker finally got the ball past him from Johnny Campbell's cross with 12 minutes remaining. As Celtic pressed forward for another goal, Souza and Lawler clashed in an incident and had to be separated by their team-mates.

In the final few minutes, Celtic forced three corners and seemed to have scrambled an equaliser, but the effort was ruled offside and at full-time Celtic accepted the 2–1 defeat by the better team. Joe Douglas replaced the injured Mick O'Flanagan in the second half.

The game attracted a crowd of 3,651 which was fewer than for the visits of Liverpool to Fall River Stadium in 1946 and 1948.

In the next morning's edition of the *Fall River, Mass, Herald News*, the sports editor, Frank McGrath, ran a story below Herman Mello's match report on a series of disputes which almost prevented the game from taking place.

> Two incidents which preceded the start of last night's international soccer game at Fall River Stadium between Belfast Celtic and New England All-Stars caused Joe Madowsky, promoter of the game, to arrange a conference in New York, Sunday, with John J. Barriskill, executive secretary of the United States Soccer Football Association, and Erno Schwartz, business manager of the American Soccer League.
>
> Fifteen minutes before last night's game was scheduled to start, according to Madowsky, he was told by William Morrissette, president of the Southern New England Football Association that he (Morrissette) could stop the game from going on if he so desired.
>
> Surprised at the statement, Madowsky asked the reason for it and was told that he had not obtained permission from the SNEFA to play the game.
>
> The promoter said that he had the permission of the USSFA, the national governing body of soccer, to play the game and added that he didn't realise he had to have the sanction of the SNEFA.

Then, according to the promoter, he asked Morrissette why he had waited until 15 minutes before game time to make such an announcement when he could have told Madowsky on any of his several visits to the Stadium box office in the past two weeks.

Morrissette replied that it was his (Madowsky's) business to know the rules.

The SNEFA head then stated, said Madowsky, that he wouldn't be mean enough to prevent the game but made it plain that he had the authority to do so.

Morrissette then informed Madowsky that a group of referees wanted to be given free admission to the game. Vincent Costa, USSFA financial delegate to the game, and Morrissette agreed that they had no jurisdiction in the matter and told Madowsky that it was entirely up to him.

Madowsky then informed Morrissette that he would not submit to the demands of the referees for they were spectators and should pay as well as any other spectator.

The next development, said Madowsky, was a statement by one of the game officials, whom he identified as Joe Amaral, that he would not work as linesman unless all referees outside the grounds were admitted free.

Amaral then left the Stadium but Madowsky went after him and induced him to return. The promoter told Amaral that he was willing to leave the question of free admission for referees to a decision by the USSFA but in the meanwhile they would have to buy tickets if they wanted to see the game. If the USSFA ruled that the referees were entitled to free admission, their money would be refunded, explained Madowsky.

At this point, John Grygiel, assigned to the game as a linesman, walked out of the grounds, carrying a bag containing his equipment.

According to Madowsky, Morrissette warned Grygiel that his action might mean suspension; the official replied that he didn't care if he was suspended for life.

Madowsky then gave up the struggle and told Morrissette to take over the gate and admit all the referees in the group.

After the game, which started about half an hour late, Madowsky said he was not fighting for the comparatively few dollars involved but for the principle.

He still doesn't think the referees not assigned to the game have any right to demand free admission but is willing to abide by a ruling of the USSFA.

A witness to the unscheduled proceedings at the stadium was William Black, secretary of the Kearny New Jersey Celtics of the American Soccer League and one of the local league delegates at last night's game. The other league delegate was Anthony Davidson, manager of the Kearny Celtics. Black said that in his opinion the referees were entirely wrong in their action last night. He explained that when such exhibitions are played in New York and New Jersey, a referees' association requests free admission for its members several days in advance of the game.

The request is granted, said Black, but on condition the head of the referees' association is stationed at the gate to identify the referees.

He added, however, that the question of free admission for referees is entirely up to the promoter. A game with the touring Scottish team is scheduled here 15 June. But before he goes ahead with any definite arrangements, Madowsky wants a few questions answered. He doesn't intend, he said, to go through any more such experiences as he had last night – hence his decision to visit New York and confer with Barriskill and Schwartz.

The next game in the Celtic tour was scheduled for Sunday, 22 May at Triborough Stadium where Scotland were also due to play in the double header. But torrential rain forced the games to be postponed. Belfast Celtic moved on to Philadelphia's Yellowjacket Stadium on Wednesday, 25 May for the game against the Philadelphia All-Stars where Harry Walker led by example as Celtic won 6–4 in the ten-goal thriller before a crowd of 3,000.

Ray McFaul put the All-Stars in front in the seventh minute and McMillen equalised direct from a free kick which completely deceived goalkeeper, Gill Schuerholz. The tide turned within the half hour as Walker drilled in the first of his two goals. Joe Douglas,

Johnny Campbell and Jim Murdough completed the Celtic scoring. The All-Stars kept in touch through Kropfelder, Valtin and Reid.

That win restored Celtic's confidence and it quietly prepared for the game against Scotland the following Sunday. Mick O'Flanagan had recovered from a strain, but Elisha Scott was forced to leave out Johnny Denver and George Hazlett who were still carrying injuries. The teams travelled together to the game at Triborough Stadium and, as they lined up behind the Scots' War Vets of America Pipe Band for the parade, the Scotland captain, George Young, said to Harry Walker, 'Harry, I hope you can give us a good game today.'

Celtic's plans had already been laid. George Hazlett knew all the Scottish players, particularly Bobby Evans, a colleague from his time at Glasgow Celtic. 'I was able to tell Elisha Scott and Harry Walker what kind of tactics to expect from Scotland and it worked,' says Hazlett. 'There's no question of Scottish pride, we wanted to beat them that day.'

The rain and gusty winds did not help Scotland settle. The ferocity of the Celtic tackling was unnerving and, within the first minute, Young got an early indication of what kind of game it would be as Dorman burst through on the right and Johnny Campbell went close with a header. But Campbell made amends when he gave Celtic the lead after 27 minutes as the Scottish defence got itself in a mix-up and left goalkeeper Brown unable to prevent the score. The interval team talk from Elisha Scott and Harry Walker fired up Celtic for the second half.

'We told the players that Scotland were not invincible and that we could beat them,' recalled Walker. 'You could see the boys growing in confidence the longer we kept Scotland at bay. You could feel everyone being boosted by it.'

Within ten minutes of the restart Scotland was left shell-shocked as Moore forced a Campbell shot over the line to make it 2–0 and the British champions realised the strong possibility of defeat.

'That second goal was originally credited to Johnny Campbell, but his shot stopped short of the line and Alex Moore finished it off,' said Harry Walker many years afterwards, anxious to clear up the confusion regarding the goal scorer.

'None of us really cared about who scored. When we won, it was the most marvellous feeling,' recalls Johnny Denver, who watched from the sidelines. 'After the game we travelled back to the hotel together and had great fun on the bus singing lots of Irish songs. Scotland didn't join in.'

'We were celebrating and that night New York was really alive. We assumed that Scotland had an early night to bed. We didn't see any of them about.'

After losing to Belfast Celtic, Scotland stated that following this defeat there would never again be another game against a club side. Mick O'Flanagan, the dual Irish rugby and football international who played as an amateur with Bohemians, had joined the Belfast Celtic tour as a replacement for the injured Jimmy Jones. Nearly fifty years later, the game against Scotland remains vivid in his memory.

'I was very offended by the behaviour of some of the Scotland team. Some started to make sectarian comments about Catholics and Papist bastards. Naturally they were annoyed and disappointed and felt that they had let themselves down, but even so, I was shocked by the things that were being said. I'd never experienced that sort of religious bigotry.

'George Young, their captain, later tried to play down the significance of the result by saying that it was only an exhibition game and that we had been taking it too seriously.'

During the second half, O'Flanagan and Willie Waddell were involved in a fight and it took several minutes to restore order before play could continue. Bud Aherne and Bobby Evans also got drawn into a confrontation as tempers deteriorated. The result marked Scotland's first defeat on North American soil since 1927 and sports writer Erwin Single, of the *World's Sports Extra*, described it as the biggest upset on the soccer horizon that year.

> The Belfast Celtics, a team rated several notches below international standards, had turned the trick before 15,000 startled Scots and Irish Americans who couldn't believe their eyes.
>
> Far from proving that Belfast is a better team than the famed Scottish Internationalists, it nonetheless proves that no International team of repute can afford to gamble in an exhibition against a club team such as Belfast. The US promoters of the Scottish Team's tour had tried in vain to get Scotland to permit its team to play against either Newcastle United or Kamraterna Gotenborg, both of whom will be in New York at the same time. The Belfast game was a compromise and expected to be an easy victory for the Kilties.

The teams were:

Belfast Celtic: McAlinden, McMillan, Aherne, Walker, Currie, Lawler, Moore, Dorman, Campbell, O'Flanagan, Bonnar.

Scotland: Brown, Govan, Young, Evans, Telfer, Cox, Waddell, Redpath, Thornton, Steel, McKenzie.

Following the historic win against Scotland, both teams were back at Triborough Stadium within 24 hours for the rearranged games which had been rained off on 22 May.

Belfast Celtic opened proceedings with a 3–3 draw against the Philadelphia Nationals. Former Baltimore star Nick Kropfelder finished off a right-wing cross from Tom Oliver to give the Nationals the lead after 25 minutes. Kropfelder set up Oliver five minutes later to stretch that advantage. The half-time talk must have spurred Belfast Celtic out of their lethargy. A lengthy assault on the Nationals penalty area was rewarded when Paddy Bonnar fired a shot past the stranded goalkeeper, Gill Schuerholz. But Philadelphia responded almost immediately as McFaul fed the ball to Kropfelder to score his second goal of the game. Celtic refused to panic and its patience was rewarded when Harry Walker capitalised on a defensive mix-up to reduce the score to 3–2. The pressure for an equaliser finally paid off with 11 minutes remaining. Alex Moore attacked up the right wing and Walker's timing proved to be perfect as he met the cross to head the ball past Schuerholz.

The 15,000-strong crowd stayed on to watch Scotland pick itself up from the shock of losing to the Irish to go on to defeat the American League 4–1. Willie Houliston, Bill Thornton, Bill Steel and Bobby Evans scored for the Scots. George McCann replied for the American League.

Belfast Celtic travelled to Canada for a second time where it outclassed a Montreal All-Stars side 4–1 in front of an estimated 10,000 spectators on 1 June. Harry Walker and Paddy Bonnar scored in the first half. Johnny Campbell and Mick O'Flanagan added two more in the second half and Montreal's McMahon hit a consolation goal for the home side.

Four days later, 4,000 spectators watched Belfast Celtic's exhibition display against the Dave Kennedy Detroit select at the University of Detroit Stadium. Celtic easily won the game 4–2.

Johnny Campbell (two), Paddy Bonnar and George Hazlett were the marksmen. Vagnetti and Morales scored for Detroit.

At the post-match press conference, Belfast Celtic chairman Austin Donnelly explained why the team appeared to stop trying to add to its goal tally against the inferior opposition.

'The object of this visit to Detroit is to help the game and demonstrate how it should be played,' he stated. 'We don't believe in showing up our American opponents who have treated us so royally on this trip. It would be the same if one of your good baseball teams came over to play us – they wouldn't want to embarrass us, either,' added Donnelly.

Belfast Celtic's departure from football was not to be a winning one. Perhaps it was the weariness of the long season, the American tour or the impending journey home into obscurity. At Randall's Island on 12 June 1949, 12,000 spectators witnessed Celtic's last game, where Kamraterna of Gotenborg, freshly arrived in America, won 3–0. The Swedes swept in front when Arne Nyberg beat Kevin McAlinden in the 19th minute. Sven Sjolbolm headed the second in the 46th minute and with 5 minutes remaining, Dan Ekner was set up by Nyberg to grab the third.

Two days later, the Belfast Celtic party was waving farewell to the Statue of Liberty from the decks of the *Mauretania* as she set an easterly course for Cobh. The tour had been deemed a great success. The club had won six of the ten games, drawn two and lost the other two. In scoring 30 goals and conceding 17, Belfast Celtic had lived up to its reputation as an exciting, attacking team and the scalp of Scotland had been the best prize of all.

But in all the sports coverage of the tour there appears not to have been any knowledge of the biggest story of all. None of the American media seemed to pick up on the fact that the best club side in Ireland was leaving football. Much of what was written in advance of the visit appears to have come from prepared information supplied by the club or the organisers. There are no references to the Jimmy Jones incident other than to say that he had an injured leg and had been unable to make the journey.

If this was deliberate, why? Could it have been that the organisers feared that matches would not be such a public attraction if it were known that these champions from Ireland were about to close down? Yet a paper such as the *Irish Echo*, whose editor had carried a tricolour flag with Elisha Scott before the first game of the tour, would have seen the news potential. It was a staunchly nationalist–republican newspaper appealing to the expatriate population and could certainly have exploited the story of the football club from nationalist West Belfast which had been so badly treated in Unionist-dominated Northern Ireland.

When the players returned to Belfast they went their own ways. Tom Dorman, Chappie Moore and James Murdough returned to their own Irish League clubs. Paddy Bonnar, Johnny Campbell, Robin Lawler and Bud Aherne were now committed to English football clubs.

'It was very sad saying farewell to Bud,' recalled Harry Walker. 'He came from Limerick and on the journey up from Cork, the train stopped at Limerick Junction. I remember him standing on the platform with his luggage as the train pulled out and us, hanging out the windows, waving goodbye to him.

'The rest of us were still Belfast Celtic players and as the new football season approached, the directors worked it well for themselves by getting transfer fees for those still on the club's books. They were good businessmen, right to the end.'

Belfast Celtic's North American Tour: May – June 1949

8 May	Belfast Celtic 2	New York All-Stars 2	(New York)
	Bonnar	Villanon	
	Denver	Chacurian	
12 May	Belfast Celtic 5	Ulster United 0	(Toronto)
	Hazlett (2)		
	Dorman		
	O'Flanagan		
	Campbell		
14 May	Belfast Celtic 3	New Jersey Stars 0	(New Jersey)
	Campbell		
	Dorman		
	Moore		

18 May	Belfast Celtic 1	New England All-Stars 2	(Fall River)
	Walker	Millington	
		Almeida	

25 May	Belfast Celtic 6	Philadelphia All-Stars 4	(Philadelphia)
	Walker (2)	McFaul	
	McMillan	Kropfelder	
	Douglas	Valtin	
	Campbell	Reid	
	Murdough		

29 May	Belfast Celtic 2	Scotland 0	(New York)
	Campbell		
	Moore		

30 May	Belfast Celtic 3	Philadelphia Nationals 3	(New York)
	Walker (2)	Kropfelder (2)	
	Campbell	Oliver	

1 June	Belfast Celtic 4	Montreal All-Stars 1	(Montreal)
	Walker	McMahon	
	Bonnar		
	Campbell		
	O'Flanagan		

5 June	Belfast Celtic 4	Detroit Select 2	(Detroit)
	Campbell (2)	Vagnetti	
	Bonnar	Morales	
	Hazlett		

12 June	Belfast Celtic 0	Kamraterna–Sweden 3	(New York)
		Nyberg	
		Sjoblom	
		Ekner	

TEN

LIVING IN HOPE

Life went on after Belfast Celtic's withdrawal from the Irish League. The new season kicked off with Crusaders taking their place along with some of their players who had had their registrations transferred to the Shore Road club. Linfield won the Championship after a play-off with Glentoran, while Crusaders finished second from bottom. But questions still remained unanswered about the manner of Celtic's departure from football and, in the intervening years, rumours have developed into theories.

There have been suggestions that a boardroom dispute concerning the ownership of shares and the appointment of directors had been rumbling for some time before the Jimmy Jones incident on Boxing Day, 1948. The rumour mill reported that the riot at Windsor Park presented the Celtic irectors with the chance they had been waiting for to pull out. The company minutes for the crucial period in question are missing and one can only speculate on what the board of directors was considering.

It may well be that the affairs of the club were not run with the same enthusiasm following the death of its secretary Bob Barr in May 1947, but suggestions of a dispute over the appointment of one of his family to the board seems less than certain. Barr had four sons. Two of them were dentists and the other two became doctors. None appears to have had anything other than a passing interest in the fortunes of Belfast Celtic. Mary Barr, Bob Barr's widow, did hold shares in the club and, it seems, raised occasional objections to some of the dealings of the club.

Despite Celtic's withdrawal from football, greyhound racing continued to be organised at Celtic Park by a leasing company. While there were boardroom differences between those who favoured the greyhound racing and those who saw football as being the priority, these were not regarded as sufficient reasons for pulling out of the Irish League. However, any lingering acrimony may have prevented a consensus being established which could have brought the team back to life. Sadly, the public interest in greyhounds was never able to match the days of the great football crowds and, over time, the walls and gates of Paradise began to fall into disrepair.

'The decision wasn't based purely on Celtic's view of the Jimmy Jones incident. It was the culmination of a number of things and how the club felt it was being treated by the football authorities. That riot was, if you like, the straw that broke the camel's back,' says Jimmy McSparran, whose family were major shareholders in the club.

'The board was made up of men who were successful outside the game. They did not look at the situation purely in terms of making money. They were genuinely worried that sectarianism was taking a hold of the game and that someone could get killed. They did not want to be responsible for that. The board was unanimous in its decision.'

While the decision to leave football was taken within weeks of the Boxing Day riot, the Celtic board, acting on the advice of agents, chose not to announce the fact immediately.

Clubs in England and Scotland were contacted and made aware that offers could be made for the leading players. It would have been poor business practice to have done otherwise. The market value of the star players could have been diminished. But was the decision to withdraw from the Irish League meant to be a permanent one? After all, there had been the other and, arguably, more serious occasion in 1920 when Celtic had gone out of the game and continued its other business activities before being persuaded to return.

'I'm not sure that it was meant to be such a permanent situation,' says Jim McSparran. 'Certainly the board took the view that the club should pull out until things improved and, while it did give consideration to a return, the time was never deemed to be right.'

There is little evidence of any immediate quest by the football authorities to attempt to broker a Celtic return. While the board was in no mood to listen, neither were the Irish Football League and the Irish FA ready to acknowledge that the game had been dealt a serious blow.

In practical terms, Celtic could not have come back into league football by itself. Another club would also have had to gain membership to keep the numbers even. As it was, Belfast Celtic had sold off its best players and re-assembling a top class team would not have been an immediate possibility.

'Many of the former Celtic players kept in close contact and there was almost an understanding that if the club had come back into the game, they would have been ready to rejoin,' says former player Jimmy Donnelly, whose move to Crusaders from Celtic included a stipulation that Celtic would receive a share of any future transfers to other clubs. However, Donnelly, using an assumed name, went south and played for Longford Town for a couple of seasons.

'Looking back it seems as if the Celtic board was waiting for some kind of an apology from the IFA which never came.'

Football was seen again at Celtic Park as Paradise opened its gates to exhibition games. On a scorching hot day on 17 May 1952, Charlie Tully led out Glasgow Celtic against a Belfast Celtic select (playing under the banner of Newry Town who were affiliated to the Irish League) in a charity game which attracted nearly 28,000 spectators.

Thoughts that this match marked the first signs of a return must have had something to do with the emotionally charged welcome which greeted the teams. Elisha Scott, in charge of the Belfast team, signalled the teams arrival on the pitch with a wave of his white hankie. Tully and Jack Vernon, captain of the Belfast team, emerged to resounding cheers and a stadium rendition of 'Auld Lang Syne'. While one large banner asked 'Will Ye No Come Back Again?', spectators took up the theme in song.

The Glasgow team, which included Jock Stein and Bertie Peacock, won the game 3–2. Kevin McAlinden was at fault for the winning score. Charlie Tully and Paddy Bonnar had under-par performances with Tully limping out of the game at half-time because of a leg injury.

Many people must have speculated about a possible return to football when they considered Elisha Scott's position. Why did he remain at Paradise where there was no team to manage and when at least one other club, Glenavon, wanted his services? Could it have been that his decision to stay at Celtic Park was due to some knowledge or belief that Belfast Celtic's return was a possibility? Is it conceivable that Belfast Celtic was contemplating affiliation to the

League of Ireland? There was a precedent for this. Alton United from the Falls League, which was affiliated to the Leinster League during the 1920s, had won the Free State Cup in 1923. In the 1980s Derry City's return to football would be by this route.

It is more likely that Elisha Scott, who died in 1959, had worsening health problems and was content to take on a caretaker's role at Celtic Park for the remaining years of his life. Billy Scott says that his father had begun to slow down. 'Don't forget that he did have a heart problem and that, after the Jimmy Jones incident, he had begun to smoke and drink a lot more than he used to.

'It was clear to me that in the last years of his life, he had become less confident about rebuilding a side. He actually dreaded the prospect.'

In his 1958 autobiography, *Passed to You,* the late Charlie Tully pointed out how much the Irish League had been affected by Belfast Celtic's absence. He pointed to the falling standard of play, the lack of competitive games and the serious loss of revenue. Tully highlighted the resolve of the club Directors not to change their minds even though Celtic had claimed the scalp of Scotland on its farewell tour to the USA.

> You'd have thought a victory like that would have induced Celtic's Directors to change their minds and have another crack at staying in the game. But they'd had enough. They had said they were quitting – and quit they did.
>
> Since then, the best playing field (outside Wembley) and the trimmest stadium (bar none) has seldom been used. When the dogs – or some exhibition game – aren't in progress, all is silent.
>
> I can tell you, as one raised in the shadow of Celtic Park, it's a depressing feeling to pass the old place and know its turnstiles are closed 'for ever' to the football fans of Belfast.

Tully wrote that on those visits home he would often call to see his old adversary, Elisha Scott.

> Elisha believes that there isn't much chance of Celtic staging a come back. But that doesn't mean to say there won't be one. There are still two of the board left – Doc

McSparran and Patsy McAlinden. And who knows what they will do.

I want to make it known in this book of mine that if ever they do return to Irish football, I'd like to play a part in that come-back as a player, coach, scout or in any other capacity. And it's not just that I'd be handy for home, either. It's because I know just how much Celtic means to Ulster. The game needs them badly. Even the Linfield supporters will tell you that. And the fans of every other club will agree with nobs on.

Celtic were always a well-managed club. They made a habit of selling two players a year – mostly to England. But there were always two reserves ready to walk in the first team.

My old club gave some star material to the English club football and to Ireland's international side. But where are those players Celtic used to discover and develop?

I say that, because Belfast Celtic no longer operate, many young local lads are lost to football. For many of them it's a case of if they cannot join the green and whites, they would rather not play for anyone. And they just drift out of football.

Any desire to resurrect Belfast Celtic in the 1950s was not helped by the IRA campaign of violence which began in 1956 and continued sporadically until 1962. While worse troubles were to afflict Northern Ireland before that decade was complete, the willingness to support a football team, so much identified with nationalism, would not have been a prerogative.

Historian Dr Eamon Phoenix suggests that Belfast Celtic's demise coincided with a period of great change for Northern Ireland. Improvements to housing and health care were to be followed by the introduction of the 1947 Education Act which would bring long-term change to the status of Catholics in Northern Ireland.

'When Belfast Celtic left football in 1949, the club could not have known what was going to develop. This was at a pivotal point in the evolution of the state and the birth of a new nationalism,' he says.

'By the 1960s and 1970s, a Catholic middle-class was emerging which wanted to unlock the doors into the civil service and the prestige professions – places where nationalists could never go before. As this middle-class realigned itself and became more remote from the working class it is arguable that Belfast Celtic might have become an embarrassment to those people.'

Within the Catholic nationalist communities in Northern Ireland, the emergence of the civil rights movement and the agitation for political change became a priority. Bringing back a defunct football club was not on any agenda.

Dr Eamon Phoenix believes that if Belfast Celtic had still been in existence when the 'Troubles' of the late 1960s began, Celtic Park could not have avoided becoming embroiled in the violence which blighted the city for several generations. 'It's inconceivable that Belfast Celtic would not have been a focus for sectarianism and attack during the recent troubles. Imagine how Celtic Park might have been exploited for anti-internment and H-Block rallies.'

On Boxing Day 1968, a fund-raising game took place at Celtic Park where Jimmy Jones scored all seven goals for a Belfast Celtic select. Over £800 was raised for the family of the late Johnny Campbell and afterwards, at a reception, some of those gathered discussed ways in which the club might return.

The family of Dan McCann, who had been chairman of the company until his death in the 1920s, had kept its share-holding in the company. His son-in-law, Dermot Hennessey, a Dublin-born businessman who was involved in sport both as a rugby referee and an administrator, was acutely aware of the potential for insurance claims against the company as Celtic Park fell into further dilapidation. Outside the ground, fencing was in danger of falling on to the Donegall Road, while inside Paradise, the situation was even worse. The club house had been completely vandalised and the concrete terracing had become a wilderness of whin bushes growing up through the concrete and hiding the rusting crash barriers.

Even though the company, Belfast Celtic Football and Athletic Company Limited, had become dormant, Hennessey joined the board during the 1970s and was later made company secretary. Northern Ireland was already under the direct rule from Westminster when Hennessey tried to persuade the Labour government to create some kind of legal structure which could have regenerated Celtic Park and transformed it into a community amenity for the people of the area – one of the principle foundations on which Celtic was established 70 years before.

Hennessey's suggestions were not accepted, but development did go ahead with the building of the nearby Olympia Leisure Centre and public playing fields at Boucher Road. It is apparent that the prospect of helping to fund any major projects in that part of the city was anathema to some influential elements within the Northern Ireland civil service. As Dermot Hennessey continued in his attempts to sort out the affairs of the company, it was unclear who was responsible for the upkeep of Celtic Park, the landlord who was Belfast Celtic Football and Athletic Co. Ltd, or the leasing tenant – the Celtic Greyhound Racing Company. Belfast Celtic was not receiving any rental income to carry out repairs.

Eventually, in 1976, Dermot Hennessey did find new owners for Celtic Park. Bookmakers Sean Graham and Jim Delargy bought a majority holding in the company following a resolution at an extraordinary general meeting where the board then recommended the offer to the shareholders.

'They didn't come in to do an asset-stripping job on the place. They spent a lot of money repairing the stand, the fences and wall. A new proper sand-based track, and a state of the art sprinkler system were installed. They had big plans for the place and were expecting a return on their investment,' says Dermot Hennessey's son, Frank, who succeeded his father as secretary.

Jim Delargy has retired from his bookmaking business but remains as chairman of Belfast Celtic and Athletic Club Ltd.

'The company held a licence to run greyhound racing at Celtic Park which was going down the tubes. Those running it had been making a living out of it, but were not prepared to put any money back into it.

'We wanted to revive greyhound racing in the city and bought Celtic Park and the other greyhound venue at Dunmore Park as well.'

After the sitting tenants had been removed from Celtic Park, the new owners spent over £600,000 on renovations and £90,000 on a new floodlighting system.

'We ran it for a few years and while the initial support was good, it was never enough to service the bank loan. The troubles got really bad and because of Celtic Park's location, it became too dangerous for people to go out at night.'

With extreme regret, Jim Delargy and Sean Graham were eventually forced to sell the 12 acres of Celtic Park to a company called Brookmount Properties in order to repay the bank loan.

'I'm convinced that if the greyhound venture had worked then football could have come back to Celtic Park as well. But that would have meant controlling the hooligans who would have been out to spoil things.'

The bulldozers moved into Belfast Celtic in 1985 and began work on what has become the Park Centre – a single-story shopping complex and car park. Dermot Hennessey died suddenly in 1982 and did not witness the final destruction of Paradise. However, Frank Hennessey recalls his last visit to the stadium.

'It was the night before Celtic Park officially closed. Even though the lights were on, it was gloomy and empty and there was a great sense of desolation. I felt very saddened by the thought that such a great sporting monument was about to be demolished.'

Even though that physical symbol of Belfast Celtic's existence has been removed from the city's landscape and the memory of the club has dimmed, it has not diminished entirely. A few of its players are still alive and many of those who remember seeing the team play, harbour ambitions of its eventual return. But could the club come back to the people it abandoned in 1949? If it did, who would finance it, where would it be based, what League could it belong to? Would it attract sufficient support to warrant the effort? Is there the danger that the sectarianism which afflicts the game in Northern Ireland and caused Celtic's departure in 1949 would strike the club again?

The Good Friday agreement that was eventually signed in Belfast on 10 April 1998 by political parties in Northern Ireland and both the Irish and British governments, is still in its embryonic stages. And as the communities in Northern Ireland search for agreement on a way in which to govern themselves, there is the tantalising prospect that long- term political stability might lead to the circumstances in which Belfast Celtic could be revived.

'I'd love to see it in my lifetime,' says Michael McGuigan, whose father Paddy was one of the trainers of Belfast Celtic. 'The city and the people need it. It's as simple as that.'

Bill McKavanagh, who lived on the Falls Road until his death in January 1998, dedicated much of the last years of his life to promoting the memory of the club with a very successful slide show which related the exploits of the club.

'Bill used to say, "When we had nothing, we had Belfast Celtic and then we had everything," and I know he would be delighted with such a prospect,' says his brother Danny, who still supports his childhood heroes.

'Celtic filled our life in those days and if the club came back, we'd be back there straight away. There are thousands of people who travel to Glasgow Celtic every week, but Belfast Celtic would give them a reason to support Irish League football again.'

In November 1998, the chairmen of the ten clubs in the Irish League's premier League met at the Irish FA's headquarters in Belfast to be presented with a discussion document entitled 'The Way Forward'. This proposal was described as a new vision for the game in Northern Ireland. It declared its future aim to provide 'an entirely new cultural environment in which Northern Ireland's foremost football clubs can improve their quality, and image, maximise the commercial value of the game and thus ensure football's long-term future and prosperity, both domestically and internationally'.

The Irish FA was acknowledging that the game is in serious decline and that steps need to be taken to revive it. There are too many competitions playing to too few spectators at sub-standard facilities. Drastic root and branch surgery is required to bring the game into the new millennium.

So could a Belfast Celtic return be part of that revival?

'Well, Irish football would be foolish not to welcome a club like Belfast Celtic back into the game,' says Irish FA president, Jim Boyce, one of the more enlightened administrators of recent years. 'I would be more than happy to give the idea my support in any way I can.'

Boyce, former chairman of Cliftonville, has long recognised the fact that senior football in Northern Ireland has not drawn enough support from the nationalist community and that there is a huge untapped pool of both potential players and followers.

'We need to do something to stem the flow of fans who now give their total allegiance to football teams in Scotland and England. It is a matter of record that the Irish FA would welcome Derry City back into its ranks. Obviously, if that were to happen, the prospect of being joined by a team of the stature of Belfast

Celtic would be attractive to all of those who are genuinely interested in the welfare and development of the game.

'Too much money has gone out of the game here. There has to be some credible planning for the future if we are to survive.'

Derry City chairman, Kevin Friel, sees no imminent return to the Irish League for the Brandywell club. It left senior football in 1971 due to the civil unrest and when it returned in 1985, it was a full member of the League of Ireland.

'A club cannot divorce itself from the area that it is based in and we would have problems with certain aspects of the Irish League. Even the return of a club such as Belfast Celtic would just have novelty value for a season and then the crowds would drop away,' says Friel.

Jim Boyce recognises that many hurdles would have to be overcome before any such idea of a Belfast Celtic return could become a reality. While he is, officially, unable to suggest how this could be achieved, it is clear that an offer of an old team bringing a new facility and a new generation of support to the game would not be ignored. The proposed structure under consideration for a new Irish FA Premier League notes that clubs 'will be invited to join'.

'All I can say to you is that when Derry City joined the League of Ireland, it did not go in at the top. It joined a lower division and was promoted very quickly. Perhaps that is a model for use again.'

Jim Boyce's football duties keep him in regular contact with what FIFA is planning. He recognises that, in the global context, continuing developments in the sport are bound to impact on both parts of the island of Ireland.

'As football evolves in the next millennium, there'll be changes over which we will have no control and we will have to adapt like every other football nation. Cooperation between the Irish FA and the FAI has never been better.'

But that level of harmony does not extend to plans for a unified national team or an all-Ireland League – yet.

'We are two independent associations and neither would support unification. It would reduce the number of players who could gain international caps and it would cut the number of clubs competing in European competition.'

Despite the re-affirmation that the football associations are not about to join forces, Boyce does want cooperation to extend to cross-border competitions. 'I would like to see the opportunity for an all-Ireland cup competition inside the next three years. That's something the football public would like to see and we must not forget their importance to the game.'

If an all-Ireland cup is in the pipeline, what else awaits us around the corner? Is there a possibility of a restructured Irish League, where the format for competition could model itself on club rugby in that the domestic Championship is played for first and is then followed by the all-Ireland League? The debate on the merits of a League in which teams such as Linfield, Glentoran, Derry City and Belfast Celtic could be playing Bohemians, Shelbourne, Cork City and St Patrick's Athletic on a regular basis is bound to be resumed.

Kevin Friel is prepared to add Derry City's view to any dialogue on the future of the game in Ireland. 'Realistically, both football associations on the island need a joint approach to the game. It must be possible to get rid of a lot of the meaningless competitions and pre-season friendlies and organise a competition encompassing both associations.'

In 1998, the prospect of a team from the English Premier League relocating to Belfast was being put forward by various interested parties. A site had been earmarked on reclaimed land on the foreshore of Belfast Lough at Duncrue, off the M2 motorway. It was being suggested that if Wimbledon could be persuaded to leave Selhurst Park, South London, the ground which it shares with Crystal Palace, then Belfast would be the ideal location.

Jim Boyce is one of many who argue against such a scheme, believing that it could cause further damage to the Irish League. 'To be honest, I think that the rebirth of Belfast Celtic offers more potential for success than the idea of bringing Wimbledon here.'

Marty Quinn, who won an Irish Cup medal with Cliftonville in 1979 and was manager of the club when it won the Irish League title in 1998 after a gap of 88 years, echoes those sentiments.

'The peace process is making inroads and the game has to look forward. Politically, the time may arrive soon where a club like Belfast Celtic could return. It could be the kick-start that the game here needs and from my point of view it would be more viable than the idea of an English premier side.

'Five years ago the idea might have been pie in the sky, but so much has happened in the past couple of years – who is to say that a Celtic side back in the Irish League in the next few seasons is an impossibility?'

Quinn, whose club is forced to operate on a meagre budget, looks enviously to the League of Ireland and how the game is developing there.

'In the north we have to try and adopt the same coaching strategies and make the game attractive to the youngsters. There is no difference in the level of ability of the kids north or south who are taking up football. The success of the south at bringing more Irish-born players through at international level shows that it can be done. In some ways the coaching facilities here in the Irish League are primitive. There are too many matches and not enough time to concentrate on the basics of coaching and skills.'

Marty Quinn is convinced that an Irish League or even an all-Ireland League which included Belfast Celtic would help regenerate the game. 'I would love to see it. The interest could be phenomenal and it could inject a lot of money into football. I'd be among the first to apply for the manager's job.'

John Walker, the son of the former Celtic captain Harry Walker, an official with the Northern Ireland Millennium Company, believes that in west Belfast there isn't any focus on football and that an urgent injection is needed to revive the game in Northern Ireland. His preferred option is for an English premiership team to play in Belfast which could renew interest and raise the playing standards in the next century.

'I think Irish League football is dead on its feet. Apart from a couple of teams, the clubs are held together by a couple of benefactors who are prepared to put money into the game because they love football.

'The statistics show that the crowds are going down and our standing in Europe is going down, while the standard elsewhere is getting better. Linfield and Glentoran get the main support a couple of times a year. You could get that with Linfield against Celtic or Glentoran against Celtic. There is a huge catchment area in west Belfast and while a few drift across to support Cliftonville, most don't appear to support any team.'

Kevin Friel is convinced that for the crowds to be tempted back to football, there will have to be better facilities which many clubs are not in a position to provide.

'Clubs, north and south, have a product to sell and if we are to get elite teams which can sustain themselves, it may reach the stage where a breakaway association from both Leagues has to be formed which can cope with the financial pressures and maximise the potential.'

And where could Belfast Celtic base itself if it were to be reconstituted?

'It would have to be somewhere in west Belfast,' says former player Jimmy Donnelly, who was one of those behind the organising of the Belfast Celtic centenary dinner in 1991. 'That's where the club was born. Anywhere else would be hard to accept.'

He reinforced that point to a government intermediary who made tentative inquiries in 1989 about the viability of a Celtic return.

'It was around the time of the reunion marking 40 years out of football. This man who made the approach said that the government was trying again to get some stability into west Belfast and wanted to get a number of Catholic business men involved in the investment.

'He even said that an area of ground at Kennedy Way had been earmarked for a stadium. I reported this back to the reunion committee, but that was all we ever heard.'

Devotees of Belfast Celtic wish that the club could return to the site at Celtic Park which is now the Park Centre. There have been suggestions that if the Park Centre were relocated to another part of west Belfast, less well served by shopping facilities, then the stadium could be rebuilt. In order for such a project to succeed, potential investors would require a feasible business plan.

'The Wimbledon for Belfast plan is quite a good template for an idea such as this,' says Michael Smyth, senior lecturer in Public Policy, Economics and Law at the University of Ulster, Jordanstown. 'There are several options that would be considered for such an undertaking.

'To begin with, access to long-term, low-interest capital for up to 30 years would be required. Support from the European Union would be vital and it might be possible to get funding from areas such as the European Peace and Reconciliation Fund. The European Investment Bank specialises in lending for infrastructural projects like this and it can syndicate loans with local banks. The EIB can offer rates of interest well below market rates.

'There would be a lot of risk capital involved, but if there was a physical asset such as a stadium, this would make things easier.'

Before any plan could proceed, an economic appraisal would assess all possible options for the project.

'Where there is public funding, a full appraisal is necessary. The benefits and costs of all the options, which include doing nothing, are assessed and discounted over the period of the long-term loan.

'The question to be answered is, which one represents the best value? On the face of it, this idea has more going for it than other projects,' adds Smyth.

Any new stadium would have to be multi-purpose to allow for other uses and potential investors would also consider the potential marketing opportunities of a new club coming back to football.

The Irish FA's document, 'The Way Forward', points out the need for clubs to provide modern facilities in their grounds and that the availability to local government funding 'will be totally dependent upon clubs having in place a sustainable programme of community involvement and development'.

A reconstructed Paradise might qualify for such funding. The Sports Council for Northern Ireland is dedicated to integrating sport into all the communities and its former chairman Don Allen, who retired in March 1999 after nine years in the post, offers a radical alternative for how Belfast Celtic could return to the community it served with distinction for 58 years.

'Why is there the need to spend a vast amount of money on a facility in that part of the city when there is Casement Park?' he says.

Casement Park, which is undergoing a multi-million-pound upgrading, is the city's main venue for Gaelic football and hurling which are under the control of the Gaelic Athletic Association. It is about two miles from the Park Centre site. However, Don Allen dismisses the obvious difficulty that his solution presents: that the GAA does not permit the playing of soccer at any of its grounds and any such decision would require a major change in its constitution.

'We are at the edge of a new beginning for the people of Northern Ireland and sport has to play its part. If the communities here are to move forward together into the next century then compromises have to be made. Surely this can be done without breaking faith with cherished traditions.

'Gaelic sport and football have long traditions in west Belfast. I remember the thousands who used to go to watch Belfast Celtic. They were just as keen on supporting Antrim in Gaelic football and hurling. If there is the chance to create the opportunity to do so again, why don't we take it?

'Sport is there for the community and, where feasible, venues must cater for multi-usage. I know of the situation where rugby and Gaelic football matches are staged at the same venue. It's all about being able to adapt to change.'

Allen is quick to stress that while part of the funding for the Casement Park refurbishment was provided by the Sports Council through Lottery and European funding, it was not a 'strings attached' arrangement. 'Not at all,' he says. 'The application for funds to improve Casement Park was treated in the same way as for a similar project at any other sporting ground. Just imagine Belfast Celtic back among its people and running out at a packed Casement Park.'

While the company Belfast Celtic Football and Athletic Co. Ltd has ceased to trade, the title is held by the family of bookmaker Sean Graham, who died in 1986.

'We have no immediate interest in investing in a new stadium or becoming involved in any Belfast Celtic revival,' says spokesman Gareth Graham. 'But if some other party does want to talk to us about the title, then we will obviously listen to them.

'This type of project would involve millions of pounds and would have to be based on a very sound business strategy. At the moment our business interests lie elsewhere.'

Whatever lies ahead, a major consideration will be the problem of sectarianism in football. The traditions on which clubs such as Linfield, Glentoran and Belfast Celtic built their history have become symbols and expressions of loyalism and nationalism. If sectarianism was a major cause behind Belfast Celtic's withdrawal from the Irish League in 1949, what is to prevent it becoming a magnet for disturbances again if the club were to reform?

'You can't give an open and shut answer to that. Ten years ago Celtic could not have come back. Linfield couldn't even play at Cliftonville. It would have been like adding gunpowder to a fire,' says John Walker. 'It's difficult to predict what lies ahead and whether it would be the same if they came back. As we get over the worst of the troubles and there is more tolerance for cultural traditions and differences, it might well succeed.'

The challenge of changing the minds of those for whom sectarian chanting and misbehaviour have become an integral part of supporting football is one of the most difficult tasks facing those who are trying to rebuild the image of the game.

'This is a disease which can be combated,' says former Northern Ireland Sports Council chairman Don Allen. 'It is a problem throughout sport though the worst examples appear to be in football.

'A large percentage of the minority community do not support the Northern Ireland international team at Windsor Park or go to see League matches because of the verbal abuse. Many, too, from the majority community won't go either because they don't want to be identified with it or want their families to be subjected to it.

'If the clubs would provide better stewarding, took a stronger line against the perpetrators and were given firmer direction by the football authorities, this die-hard majority which is spoiling the image of the game could be eradicated.'

If initiatives to rekindle Belfast Celtic fail to ignite, the ambition of ever seeing a team kit of green and white hoops playing in the Irish League again may have to rest with junior side Donegal Celtic which is situated in the Suffolk area of west Belfast. The club, which was formed in 1970, has the long-term aim of graduating to senior football. Lottery funding is available for development work at Donegal Celtic Park where there are plans to improve the playing surface, instal floodlights and provide proper facilities for up to 10,000 spectators.

'While we see ourselves as filling the space left by Belfast Celtic, we have no wish to take over its name,' states club official Andy McIlhatton. 'We have established our own identity.'

'We recognise that we appeal to the same.support and we would like to think that we could follow the old Celtic's open-door policy of using the best players whatever their religion.

'We run lots of underage teams and attract kids from all over the city. Everyone is welcome here as long as they behave.'

But Donegal Celtic's aspiration to gain a foothold on the ladder to senior football has not been served well by controversial incidents in recent seasons. An Irish Cup tie against Linfield at Windsor Park was marred by serious crowd trouble and in the 1998 Steel & Sons Cup, Donegal Celtic withdrew from the semi-final tie with the RUC team.

Initially the club had voted to play the game until it bowed to undue pressure from within its area and conceded a possible place in the Christmas morning final.

'If we gain admittance to the Irish League B division we are bound to meet the RUC at least twice a season,' explains McIlhatton. 'We are happy to play at their ground. There's no point bringing hassle down on ourselves.'

And McIlhatton gives a pragmatic view on how best to deal with the potential of sectarianism on the field or on the terracing

'We don't stand for it at our club. Anyone guilty of that is put out. We are used to the comments at other places, but we reckon that it gives us that extra incentive to respond in the best way possible – by winning.'

So perhaps the spirit of Belfast Celtic does live on and the dreams of recreating the great days of long ago may yet happen. In 1958, as Glasgow Celtic hero Charlie Tully lamented the passing of the Belfast team that had made him a celebrity, he also made a prediction.

> As I say, I've been away from Belfast for a long time, yet when I'm home visiting, I'm besieged by youngsters, hero-worshippers who would like nothing better than to support their own team and star in their own home town. I'm apparently the next best thing, though few could possibly have seen me play.
>
> Yes, it was a sorry day when Jimmy Jones was chased off Windsor Park. A sorry day for Ireland, Celtic – aye, and for the clubs who were left to play without them. They feel the pinch.
>
> Perhaps I will be allowed to make a forecast. Belfast Celtic, which has the stadium, the equipment, the organisation, the players willing to sign for them and a big support longing for the club's return to Irish football *will be back.*
>
> Speed the day!

Could that moment now be close at hand?

ELEVEN

PROFILES

THE PLAYERS

Joe Abrahams

Outside-right Joe Abrahams was signed to Belfast Celtic from
Partick Thistle in 1899 and assisted the club to its first Irish League
Championship success in 1900.

Tommy 'Bud' Aherne

Left-back Tommy Aherne was born in Limerick and began his full-
time football career with his native town in the late 1930s. He served
in the Irish Army at Fort Camden, Crosshaven, during the years of
the Second World War before joining Belfast Celtic at the age of 26
where he took over from the legendary Bertie Fulton. He stayed at
Celtic Park for four years and won a Victory international and four
senior international caps between 1946 and 1950. The last of these
was against Wales when he was playing at Luton Town, the club he
joined for £6,000 before Belfast Celtic left football. Bud also played
for the Republic of Ireland at international level and gained 16 caps
between 1946 and 1954.

Oswald Bailie

Oswald Bailie was one of Belfast Celtic's reserve goalkeepers. He had
been playing with Ards Seconds when Elisha Scott signed him in
1948. Bailie, who was from Ballymena, was a keen tennis player and
chose not to turn professional so that he could continue to be
involved in representative tennis.

His call up to the Celtic first team was unexpected. 'It was on Christmas Day 1948 against my home town team. There was no inkling at all that I was going to play until I arrived at the Showgrounds and by then I'd already eaten Christmas dinner and was stuffed with Christmas pudding.' On the field, it was Ballymena who faced a stuffing – going down 5–0.

First team choice Kevin McAlinden was being rested to allow extra time to recover from a back injury. Oswald Bailie was back on senior duty a week later when McAlinden was out injured again – this time with leg injuries inflicted by the rioting mob at Windsor Park.

'I played another seven or eight games for the first team and then I was dropped. I thought I'd done really well and went to see Harry Walker about it. He told me privately that Lish Scott had decided to leave me out of the team because he had heard I was on the verge of a junior international cap. Another senior game would have disqualified me.'

Bailie regretted that decision by Scott because in the next game Celtic were beaten 1–0 by Portadown in the Irish Cup and it was a goalkeeping error that led to the only score.

'It was a great team to play for and although it was regarded as being a Catholic club, there was no disrespect shown towards people of other religions. I was proud to be associated with Belfast Celtic and felt ashamed at the way that so-called co-religionists behaved towards them.'

Bailie offered an insight into the manager's half-time talks on one occasion when Celtic were losing 3–0 to Glentoran at the Oval. 'Lish came into the dressing-room and went for Billy McMillan and said that he wished he could have a substitute because Billy had been responsible for all three Glentoran goals. To say Scott was not very pleased is putting it mildly.'

Oswald would have loved to have gone to America with Celtic, but the club decided to use Paddy Bonnar as cover for goalkeeper Kevin McAlinden and he was not required for the farewell trip.

After his days at Belfast Celtic, Oswald Bailie moved on to play for Cliftonville, Ballymena and Distillery.

Fred Barrett

Fred Barrett played at left-back on the first Belfast Celtic team to win the Irish Cup – in 1918. He was sent off during the Irish Cup match against Glentoran, at Solitude, in 1920 when shots were fired into the crowd. Barrett transferred later to Chelsea along with Jimmy Ferris and, on returning to Belfast at the end of his career, he became the groundsman at Celtic Park. Barrett was credited with coaching Charlie Tully on the art of scoring goals directly from corner kicks.

Tommy 'Darkie' Best

The nickname would not be deemed to be appropriate in this age of political correctness, but Tommy Best's place in Belfast Celtic's history is gained by being the first black footballer to play in Irish football. He was stationed in Belfast with the Royal Navy during the war. Best, a winger, played for Celtic's second team, but did get several first team outings. His Football League career took him to Chester, Cardiff, Queens Park Rangers and Hereford.

Paddy Bonnar

Paddy Bonnar was one of Belfast Celtic's most effective left-wingers. He played for Distillery and Dublin side, St James Gate, before coming to Paradise in 1941. He was renowned for the power of his left foot shot and spectators either loved or hated him.

Paddy was convinced that he was one of the intended targets of the rampaging crowd at the end of the infamous Boxing Day game against Linfield and that, if he had not been sent off during the second half, he could have suffered a similar fate to Jimmy Jones.

'The linesman claimed that I used abusive language towards him when the ball went out of play. I didn't, but at the end of the game I was able to get away from the crowd,' he recalled many years later.

Bonnar was a member of the team that defeated Scotland in New York in 1949. Afterwards he was transferred to Barnsley and spent some time at Aldershot before returning to the Irish League for spells at Derry City and his native Ballymena.

While never receiving full international caps, he won inter-

League honours and played against England and Scotland in Victory internationals in 1946.

He was knocked down in a road accident near his beloved Paradise and died ten months later in July 1991 as a result of his injuries.

Tommy Breen

Tommy Breen was regarded as one of the outstanding goalkeepers of the twentieth century. Born in Drogheda, County Louth, he played for Belfast Celtic, Manchester United, Linfield, Shamrock Rovers and Glentoran.

Breen had been an inside-left in junior football until a leg injury caused him to take over as goalkeeper rather than miss playing. This became his favourite position and he was spotted by Newry Town where he signed, initially as an amateur, in 1929. He moved to Belfast Celtic in 1932. The first of his nine international caps was against England at Goodison Park in 1934.

Breen was transferred to Manchester United two years later and he stayed at Old Trafford until the outbreak of the Second World War. He returned to Belfast Celtic where he won an Irish Cup medal in the 1–0 defeat of Linfield in the 1941 final.

The following season, Breen moved to Windsor Park after he was unable to agree financial terms with Belfast Celtic. He was paid an extra ten shillings a week at Linfield, where he became club captain. He collected another two Irish Cup medals in 1945 and 1946 before moving on again.

Manchester United had retained his registration and were demanding £1,000 for his transfer. Linfield were not prepared to pay that amount and Tommy Breen headed to Dublin where he signed for Shamrock Rovers.

A distinguished playing career in the Irish League came to an end in September 1947 when Breen suffered a serious knee injury while playing for Glentoran against Bangor. In a claim against Glentoran Recreation Co. Ltd, under the Workmen's Compensation Act, a settlement of £175 was agreed. Breen told the Belfast Recorder, Judge Fox K.C. that he had twisted his right knee and dislocated the cartilage and was no longer able to play football. Breen's contract with Glentoran had expired.

He remained in contact with his former colleagues and told the story of how, late in the evening, before a game between Linfield and Belfast Celtic, Celtic centre-forward Liam O'Neill arrived on his doorstep in a drunken stupor. O'Neill appeared incapable of playing in such an important game in a few hours time and Breen let him sleep until morning before sobering him up with several cups of coffee. When it was time to leave for the game, Breen ordered two taxis because he did not want them to be seen arriving at the ground together. O'Neill recovered enough to play and repaid Breen's kindness by scoring two goals in Celtic's victory.

Tommy Breen died in March 1988.

Alf Bruce

Alf Bruce was a defender and was part of the side that Austin Donnelly built when Celtic returned in 1924. His appearances were curtailed by a serious back injury suffered in a game against a touring South African side. He played at Cliftonville where he won an amateur international cap against England in 1924.

Johnny Campbell

Johnny Campbell was born in Derry and his sporting talents lay in football and athletics. He was an accomplished sprinter and that turn of speed proved devastating throughout his football career. He won an Irish Cup medal in 1947 and before his transfer to Fulham in 1949 he represented the Irish League on several occasions. He scored one of Belfast Celtic's goals in the famous 2–0 victory over Scotland at Triborough Stadium on 29 May 1949.

Campbell often played at centre-forward though his favourite position was on the wing. He never enjoyed full health and died of bowel cancer in Belfast in January 1968. He was 44 years old.

Jimmy Connor

Jimmy Connor played at centre-half and had already won two caps for Ireland in 1901 when he moved from Glentoran to Belfast Celtic. He was capped a further 12 times between 1905 and 1911. Connor was an old-style centre-half who had a two-fold purpose in walking to matches in Belfast from his Downpatrick home: it added to his fitness and allowed him to spend his travel allowance on alcohol.

Connor was a member of the Belfast Celtic squad which toured to Prague and Bohemia in 1912.

Jackie Coulter

Jackie Coulter, who wore size 12 boots, was signed from Intermediate League side Dunmurry in season 1929–30 and his most memorable appearance was in a play-off game against Glentoran to decide the City Cup. Coulter, playing as a centre-forward, scored a hat-trick in that match to ensure that the trophy returned to Paradise.

He gained 11 international caps over a four-year period. The first of these was in February 1935 against England at Goodison Park. He was transferred later that year to Everton for a fee of £2,750. During his career on Merseyside, he was capped a further five times before moving on to Grimsby Town and Chelmsford. His last appearance in an Irish shirt was in Belfast on 8 October 1938. Scotland won 2–0.

The transfer to England caught all of Coulter's team mates by surprise. He had been sent off during a game at Ballymena and, while waiting for the game to finish, he was approached by an Everton official and agreed terms. The other ten Celtic players returned to the dressing-room to discover the news of his departure.

Billy Crooks

Billy Crooks was a small player who had started with St Galls before signing to Glentoran. He played with Manchester United where he won an international cap. Crooks had a spell with New Brighton before returning home in 1925 to sign for the team he had always wanted to play with.

Sammy Curran

Sammy Curran, a star of the 1920s, was spotted by Austin Donnelly while playing with juniors Woodburn. Nicknamed 'Blind Sammy', he rarely lost sight of the goal mouth, hammering in 51 goals in his first season at Paradise. Curran was renowned for having an uncanny sense of anticipation and, as a vital member of the team that dominated the Irish League championship from 1925 to 1929, Curran scored more than 170 goals for Belfast Celtic before moving to Derry City. In the 1926 Irish Cup final, his hat-trick secured the trophy in the 3–2 defeat of Linfield. At international level, he scored twice for Ireland during appearances against Wales and Scotland.

Charlie Currie

Charlie Currie was signed to Belfast Celtic from Cliftonville and played in the centre-half position for the Seconds as understudy to Jack Vernon. When Vernon was transferred to West Bromwich Albion, Currie was promoted to the first team.

Charlie was known as 'Curser Currie'.

He moved to Bradford in 1949 before coming back to work in the family headstone business at Arizona Street.

Johnny Denver

Johnny Denver was an inside-forward who joined Belfast Celtic in the mid-1940s from Lurgan side, Shankill Young Men. His career continued to blossom after Celtic left the Irish League and he played a memorable part in securing Glenavon its first League Championship, in 1952, with 42 goals.

'When I joined Belfast Celtic it was like moving into another world. I was used to changing in sheds, and going to a stadium like Celtic Park was like being at Highbury or Old Trafford,' he recalls.

Denver also had a role to play in Belfast Celtic's history. He was involved in the Boxing Day match against Linfield where his life-long friend, Jimmy Jones, was attacked. 'The tension at that game was unbearable and we took the lead when McCune took me down inside the area and Harry Walker scored the penalty kick. Then there was pandemonium when Billy Simpson equalised a couple of minutes later.

'At the end, I saw the crowd coming on to the field. George Hazlett, the inside-right, was struck on the face with a fist. When I saw this I made a run for it. Someone tried to hit me so I kicked him. I got off the field. It was everybody for themselves.'

During the North American tour, Johnny Denver did play in some of the games though he was not in the team that defeated Scotland.

'We had as much of the game as Scotland, but the difference was that we took our chances. Johnny Campbell gave us the lead in the first half, while Alex Moore had the final touches on the second goal. They both agreed afterwards that Alex put it in from Johnny's effort.'

One of the most lasting impressions that Denver has of Belfast Celtic was the club's positive attitude to each game. 'Celtic never thought about losing. When I was at Glenavon we had a good team, but we had to play the full match all-out to win anything. At Celtic, it was always a case of how many would you win by.'

George Doherty

George Doherty was a goalkeeper and joined Celtic from Derry Hibernians at Christmas 1924. He was described at the time as 'not a showy keeper, but useful'.

Jack Diffen

Goalkeeper Jack Diffen made his name with Belfast Celtic when Austin Donnelly rebuilt the team on their return to the Irish League in the mid-1920s. He won four Championship medals before moving to Shelbourne in Dublin for a season. He came back to Celtic in 1930 when Archie Heggarty was manager. Celtic finished third in the league and Diffen earned his only international cap against Wales in 1931.

During one season where Celtic had gone a number of games without conceding a goal, Diffen appeared to deliberately let the ball roll over the line when it was played back to him. He is alleged to have told his defenders 'You're supposed to be playing *that* way, not *this*.'

Joe Douglas

Joe Douglas, who came from the staunchly loyalist Glenmachen Street in the Village district of Belfast, was naturally apprehensive when he was signed by Celtic.

'I was worried about how I would be accepted by the team when I arrived at Celtic Park from Linfield. But that didn't last very long. They were a great bunch of guys to play with,' he once said.

Douglas played as a half-back alongside Jack Vernon and Harry Walker and was awarded one international cap against England in 1947.

Joe Devlin

Joe Devlin, Belfast Celtic's long-serving trainer, had a lifetime interest in sport. He was keen on hurling, football, athletics and boxing. In 1913 he began a 35-year association with Celtic Park when he came to train the team under-manager Jimmy McGowan.

When Celtic withdrew from football in 1920, Devlin packed his bags and headed for New York where he pursued a successful career training boxers for tournaments at Madison Square Gardens.

On Celtic's return to the game in 1924, Devlin agreed to come back as well to work for new manager Austin Donnelly. Pre-season training was under way by the time his delayed sailing across the Atlantic docked in Derry.

Devlin was 64 years old when Celtic withdrew in 1949. He did not travel to the USA as a member of the official party. That honour was given to his assistant, Paddy McGuigan.

After Belfast Celtic left football, Joe Devlin continued to operate a masseur business for sports people from his premises on the Falls Road.

John Feenan

John Feenan was a defender who came to Belfast Celtic from Newry Town in the transfer deal that included goalkeeper Tommy Breen. Feenan was sold to Sunderland in 1936.

Bob Ferguson

Bob Ferguson was a member of the 1925–6 Championship-winning team. He was a hard-tackling defender who had played with Trojans in the Falls League and then Dundela before moving from east Belfast.

Jimmy Ferris

Transferred to Chelsea in 1920 when Belfast Celtic withdrew from the Irish League, Jimmy Ferris did eventually return to Celtic Park. His playing career ended prematurely in 1930 when he was diagnosed as suffering from a heart condition. He became a scout for Celtic and was credited with persuading Davy 'Boy' Martin to come to Paradise. He was capped five times for Ireland between 1920 and 1928.

In 1925, he was described in the *Irish News* as the 'neatest and daintiest footballer in this city. His bright-coloured headpiece was always noticeable in last season's matches wherever the fight was thickest. A brilliant schemer who makes golden opportunities for his partners, he hit it off splendidly with Billy Crooks and Sam Curran.'

Bertie Fulton

Bertie Fulton was regarded as one of the great footballers of the twentieth century. Born in Larne in November 1906, he was inspired by the footballing skills of Mickey Hamill and joined Belfast Celtic in 1924 as an 18-year-old. He played at Paradise for a year before going to London to train as a school-teacher. While studying at Strawberry Hill college, Fulton joined a leading amateur team – London Caledonians – and on returning to his home town to begin his teaching career, Fulton signed for Larne. In the season 1928-9 the young full-back was back at Paradise where he played the best football of a long, distinguished career.

His last Irish Cup final appearance was in the 1943 win against Glentoran and when Bertie left Belfast Celtic, Bud Aherne took over the left-back position. Bertie Fulton went back to play for Larne before becoming coach to Celtic's second eleven.

He remained an amateur during his playing career and resisted many attempts to turn professional. 'Manchester United were keen to get him to Old Trafford, but he didn't want to go,' says Sean Fulton, the oldest of Bertie's children.

'I asked him if he ever regretted that decision. He said he didn't because, during his career, he got the chance to play against the best. He was a fine athlete who was able to test himself against people like Dixie Dean, Stanley Matthews and Len Baston.'

Bertie Fulton received many opportunities to prove his own worth. He became the highest capped Belfast Celtic player behind Elisha Scott, representing Ireland 20 times at international level. He also won numerous amateur caps between 1926 and 1938 and there would have been more if he had been given time off work to play in the mid-week games. And at the time that the political climate was changing in Europe, Bertie Fulton travelled with the Great Britain squad to Germany to compete in the 1936 Berlin Olympics.

Bertie Fulton was renowned for his speed, pace, balance and defensive abilities which contained the skills of forwards as famous as Stanley Matthews.

Sean Fulton supports the view that his father, rather than Elisha Scott, was the real tactical brain behind Belfast Celtic's success. 'Dad's objective, always, was to win. He didn't like to lose. He was far-sighted in his thinking and in the 1930s he had Celtic playing with four forwards and one winger long before others thought about it.

'I haven't heard of anyone who had the kind of tactical interest which he had. The team would let Lish, as manager, go through the basics and then Bertie would lay down the tactics.'

When there is conversation about Belfast Celtic, Bertie Fulton is one of the first names mentioned. He was held in very high regard both on and off the field.

'Bertie's play was complemented by having Harry Walker at right-half. They were a great steadying force together. When everyone else was getting excited, they would calm things down.'

Fulton did score as well – a last-minute winner in an amateur international against England when a free kick rebounded to him.

Ron Greenwood

Ron Greenwood was one of very few members of the Services to be associated with Belfast Celtic during the years of the Second World

War. Greenwood was stationed with the RAF in Maghera and was invited to play for Celtic's second eleven. He was unable to displace the ever-consistent Jackie Vernon in the first team, although he did make six first team appearances when Vernon was injured. On his return to London, Greenwood played for Chelsea and West Ham before periods as manager of the Hammers and England.

Mickey Hamill

Mickey Hamill's career with Belfast Celtic spanned 20 years and was interspersed with periods in Manchester, Glasgow and the USA. However, the lure of his native Belfast always drew him home, and back to Celtic Park, where he won five Championship and four Irish Cup medals. He also holds the unique record of winning Irish, English and Scottish Championship medals. He was a member of the Manchester United team which won the First Division title in 1911 and then, guesting with Glasgow Celtic, was a member of their title-winning squad before the Great War. Hamill retired from playing at the age of 40 to run his own pub on the Falls Road, though he did some coaching at Celtic Park.

He was drowned in a tragic accident in the River Lagan in July 1943.

George Hazlett

George Hazlett arrived from Glasgow Celtic in 1948 at the persuasion of Harry Walker who had been in Glasgow searching for new players. Hazlett, at Parkhead since his schoolboy days, had been out of the game for several months because of a persistent knee injury. 'Harry told me about their physio, Joe Devlin who could fix anything. And he did. After that, I was hardly out of the team.'

Hazlett was aware of the reputation that Belfast Celtic had throughout Britain. 'There was no doubt the club could have held its own in the Scottish League or Football League.'

George was delighted with his new surroundings and settled into digs in the Beechmount district where Robin Lawler also roomed. 'That was with a family called Curran and there was an old grandfather who used to take me to watch the boxing at the Kings Hall and the Ulster Hall. I was treated really well. The wages were good – about £10 or £12 a week, and a job to go with it. Belfast was so like Glasgow that I wasn't home sick.'

Hazlett played in the 1948 Boxing Day match and feels he was lucky not to have been seriously injured when a section of the crowd attacked the Celtic players.

'Being from Glasgow, I was a bit streetwise when it came to recognising trouble. I knew things were going to turn nasty – especially when the 'B' Specials surrounding the pitch joined in the celebrations after Linfield equalised.

'The attack on Jimmy Jones was disgraceful. He was an Alan Shearer type of player who could score goals from anywhere. That injury robbed him of the chance of becoming one of the top players in the world.'

Hazlett's knowledge of the Scottish scene helped immensely when Belfast Celtic defeated Scotland in New York in May 1949. 'We were better prepared than they were. They knew very little about our team or how we played, but I was able to tell Elisha Scott what to expect from them. My one regret is that I was injured and couldn't play in that game.'

Hazlett was transferred to Bury in 1949 and, in later years, became a qualified FA coach.

Eddie Inch

Eddie Inch was a hard-tackling half-back who played for Celtic during the Austin Donnelly reign. He helped Celtic in its resurgence in 1925 when it won four League titles in a row.

Jimmy Jones

Jimmy Jones, one of the greatest of the Belfast Celtic centre-forwards, had once been a Linfield player. They failed to recognise his potential and, despite later attempts to lure him away from Celtic Park, Jones refused. He felt that Linfield secretary Joe Mackey held a grudge against him which was to prove to have serious consequences.

'Joe Mackey's announcement at half-time about the injury to Bob Bryson turned the crowd against me in that match against Linfield on Boxing Day 1948. It's something that I won't forget. It was one of the lowest points of my football life and changed things immensely as far as I was concerned. From being a player who could have played in England for many years – at least that's what I was led to believe at the time – it just finished up with me playing the rest of my career in the Irish League.'

Jones had come to Belfast Celtic from Shankill Young Men in Lurgan and proved to be an instant success with the club. 'I was 18 when I joined them and it was marvellous to be on the same pitch as some of the big names, never mind play with them. I was rubbing shoulders with some of the all-time greats.'

In his last season at Belfast Celtic, Jones scored 30 goals in 20 matches before sustaining the serious leg injury which almost ended his career. In a subsequent court case for compensation, it emerged that Jones had been valued at £16,000 and that Newcastle United had been interested in signing him.

It took two years for him to recover from that broken leg and he was the last player on Celtic's book. A move to Fulham ran into difficulties over the issue of his registration and whether the Football Association would accept it.

When Belfast Celtic confirmed that Jones was free to sign for any club, it sparked a huge degree of interest.

'One of them, unfortunately, was Manchester United and I would say now that it was Matt Busby who caused any problems there were between the Football League, Fulham and myself.

'Unfortunately, I didn't have the finance to take legal action against the Football League. If I could have done that, I would have gained considerably and probably be a lot wealthier today.'

Jones returned to play in the Irish League where he gained international recognition and became a cult figure at his home town club Glenavon. In a 12-year period between 1950 and 1962 Jimmy Jones scored 484 goals.

'I would say that Linfield, and Irish football, were the losers without Belfast Celtic. Celtic attracted the crowds as indeed did Linfield. But when Celtic went out that was half of the cake gone. The crowds and the revenue went down. No other club in the Irish League could compensate for that. They just lost that level of support which followed them everywhere.'

Joe Kane

Joe Kane joined Celtic from Oldpark in 1925. He was used as a reserve centre-half and was able to step into the breech when needed. Barn United tried to sign him, but he preferred to stay with Celtic.

Artie Kelly

Artie Kelly came from Ligonel, Belfast, and played in the forward line in the 1940s.

Hugh Kelly

Hugh Kelly joined Belfast Celtic from Glenavon in 1941 following a spell with Chesterfield. Kelly was working in the family drapery business in Lurgan where he played Gaelic football with his local team, Clan na Gael. When he began to play football, his ball-handling skills were noticed by Glenavon manager Andy Wylie who persuaded him to take over from the injured goalkeeper in a Mid-Ulster League game. After that performance, the position became his own and Kelly made his debut in the Irish League early in 1937.

Hugh Kelly played for Belfast Celtic in the Regional League before moving on to Fulham and Southampton. His career at Celtic Park was marred by a contractual dispute which took some time to resolve. He won four international caps between 1950 and 1951. His least memorable game was against Belfast Celtic in January 1941 when he kept goal for Glenavon in the 13–0 defeat at Mourneview Park. Peter O'Connor scored 11 of them to set an individual record in Britain and Ireland.

One of the legendary stories about Hugh Kelly concerned his response to a reprimand from Belfast Celtic manager Elisha Scott. In the dressing-room after the game, Scott told Kelly, 'My grandmother could have played better out there.'

On the following Thursday evening, after training, the team sheet was posted for the next game and, as Scott was leaving the ground, he noticed that Kelly's name had been scrubbed out and replaced with the words: 'Lish's granny'.

Hugh Kelly died in Lurgan in September 1977, at the age of 56.

Norman Kernaghan

When Norman Kernaghan won his first cap for Ireland against Wales as a 17-year-old on 11 March 1936, he was the youngest ever international. That record stood for 45 years until Manchester United's Norman Whiteside played for Northern Ireland at the World Cup finals in 1982. That first game was played on a Wednesday afternoon and, in the morning, the teenage Kernaghan had gone to work as usual at the daily *Newsletter* where he was employed as a compositor.

'James Henderson, the big noise in the *Newsletter* at the time, was wandering through the newsroom and came to where I was. He said, "Kernaghan, what are you doing in here?"

"I'm at my work, sir."

He said, "Get away home and rest. You have this big game in the afternoon."

So I went home and then joined the team for lunch.'

Kernaghan scored in Ireland's 3–2 win. Elisha Scott, his manager at Belfast Celtic, made his final international appearance in that game at the age of 42.

Norman Kernaghan came from Daisyfield Street, off the Crumlin Road and had already gained amateur international caps at Cliftonville, when he joined Belfast Celtic in 1934.

He was a diminutive winger who was easily recognised by his red curly hair. Team mates nicknamed him 'Twinkle Toes' because of the silky skills which in one season brought him 54 goals. Linfield supporters were less kind in calling him 'Shirley' after the film star, Shirley Temple.

The leadership provided by Bertie Fulton and, subsequently, Harry Walker had such a profound effect on Kernaghan that he resisted offers of a football career in England with Manchester United and Huddersfield, and Hearts in Scotland.

'Fulton and Walker were great men. Bertie was older than me, and like a father to me. When you are happy and content, it's a wonderful thing. If I had gone across the water that might not have been the case. If I had been damaged and then come home, where would I have been?

'I didn't want to go away. I wanted to be here with my family and friends. I did a bit of swimming and diving. I played cricket and tennis in the summer and I was happy.'

Kernaghan played at Celtic Park until 1945 when he moved on to Distillery, Glenavon and Ballymena United. He won four Irish Cup medals, was part of the great seven-in-a-row Championship-winning sides of the 1930s and was capped three times for Ireland. In one game for Belfast Celtic, Kernaghan scored a hat-trick in four minutes against Larne, who were leading 3–1.

Billy Kirkwood

Billy Kirkwood joined Celtic from Ligoniel and was regarded as a very agile 12-stone centre-half. He played during Celtic's first season back from exile.

Robin Lawler

Joseph 'Robin' Lawler played at wing-half for Belfast Celtic following his transfer from Dublin club, Drumcondra, in 1945. He was totally committed to the game and opposing defences greatly feared his ability to throw in the ball from long distances.

'A throw-in from Robin was like receiving a free kick or a corner kick. His arms were like windmills,' remembers Harry Walker.

Lawler first came north as an 18-year-old in 1943 when he signed for Distillery and stayed for a season and a half.

He received hate mail prior to Belfast Celtic's Boxing Day game against Linfield in 1948. 'Robin was in such a state that day that I asked Elisha Scott not to play him. Robin was even trembling before he went out on to the field and I think the match was a nightmare for him until it finished,' recalled Walker.

Although Fulham had signed Lawler in March 1949 along with Johnny Campbell, both were allowed to go on Celtic's tour of North America.

Robin Lawler, who was a butcher by trade, gained eight international caps for the Republic of Ireland between 1953 and 1956. He died in London's Charing Cross Hospital on 17 April 1998, aged 72.

Tommy Lavery

Tommy Lavery played at right-back at Celtic Park and was promoted to the first team when John Feenan was transferred to Sunderland in 1936. He had worked his way through from the Seconds and partnered Billy McMillan in the full-back line in the County Antrim Shield Final of 1936 where Celtic Seconds went down 1–0 to Belfast Celtic.

Jack Leathem

Jack 'The Hack' Leathem joined Belfast Celtic in 1936 following a search for new footballing talent by Elisha Scott. The Lurgan-based player slotted into the defence almost immediately and held on to the centre-half position for several seasons until he was succeeded by Jack Vernon.

Jack Leathem was capped against Wales in Wrexham on 15 March 1939. He won three Irish Cup medals with Celtic in 1937, 1938 and 1941 as well as League Championship honours on five occasions.

Jackie Mahood

Jackie Mahood was the younger of the two talented footballing brothers. He played on the left wing for Belfast Celtic in the late 1920s where he wreaked havoc among opposing defences as Celtic steam-rolled its way to four consecutive League titles. He also won an Irish Cup medal in the 1926 final defeat of Linfield and scored for Celtic in the 1927 final. Ballymena United won that game 2–1.

The Mahoods moved from Banbridge to the Linfield heartland of Belfast's Lisburn Road and, even as an old man, Jackie remembered some of the hardship that was caused by playing at Paradise.

'We used to take a lot of abuse because we played for Celtic. I would have loved to have been a Linfield player, but the chance didn't come along and once I was at Celtic Park, I never regretted it. We were treated very fairly there.

'Celtic was such an exciting team to play for. We were virtually unbeatable and that didn't go down well. I'm sure that if I had been with the Blues, I would have been able to get more work as a plater at the shipyard. But it was held against me. That made the games against Linfield all the more special, especially when we beat them.'

Jackie Mahood played with Glentoran and Bangor before he and Stanley were signed by Austin Donnelly in 1924.

Jackie, who was Celtic's top scorer for three seasons, won nine full international caps and two amateur caps between 1925 and 1934. He scored for Ireland in the 2–0 win against England in Belfast on Saturday, 22 October 1927.

His career came to an end after suffering a broken leg in a tragic accident while playing for Ballymena United against Celtic during the 1934–5 season.

Stanley Mahood

Stanley Mahood was as effective a footballer as his much smaller brother. While the recognition Stanley received at amateur international level did not extend to full senior honours, he certainly made an impression on Belfast Celtic supporters by scoring over 100 goals from his inside-forward position.

He was a member of the squad that won five trophies in the 1925–6 season. On top of the League and Cup double, Stanley scored one of the goals in Celtic's Gold Cup final win against Cliftonville – his brother Jackie also scored.

Stanley moved to Derry City from Belfast Celtic and was later reunited with Jackie at Ballymena United.

Davy 'Boy' Martin

Davy 'Boy' Martin gained his nickname when he joined the Royal Ulster Rifles regiment as a drummer boy. There he began to make a name for himself as a centre-forward. He was able to buy himself out of the Army and after a spell at Cliftonville, he signed for Belfast Celtic on amateur forms. He did eventually turn professional and his personal tally of 36 League goals helped Celtic to its 1933 Championship title.

Davy Martin was transferred to Wolves in December 1934 along with Johnny Brown for a joint fee of £7,500. It was a huge transfer fee at the time and Martin's valuation was estimated to be £6,000.

Martin was awarded ten international caps between 1934 and

1939. He was playing in Nottingham, first for Forest and then for Notts County when the Second World War was declared. Davy re-enlisted in the Royal Ulster Rifles, played with Glentoran and was severely injured during the invasion of Normandy in 1944. After the war, he coached at Ballymena United and Carrick Rangers. He died in 1991 aged 77.

Jimmy McAlinden

Inside-forward Jimmy McAlinden was the only Belfast Celtic player ever to win an FA Cup medal. He achieved this honour within six months of leaving his beloved Celtic to join Portsmouth in December 1938 for a record transfer fee of £7,500. Portsmouth surprised Wolves 4–1 in the 1939 final at Wembley.

McAlinden was acknowledged to be one of the fastest players in the Irish League when, in 1934, he signed for the club which he had supported all his life. Belfast Celtic officials, realising that there was such a talented player living so close to Paradise, also moved quickly to sign McAlinden when he played for Glentoran Seconds against Celtic Seconds.

'You could say they had no trouble signing me. It was my boyhood dream to be a Belfast Celtic player. I started with £2. It went up to £2.50 and finished up at £3.50 in 1938-9. Back then that was big money for a 16-year-old. It was great getting paid for something you would have done for nothing anyway.'

McAlinden, who did not have any other job, trained as a full-time professional three or four mornings a week and developed his skills alongside his playing heroes Norman Kernaghan and Harry Walker.

'With Harry at the back and Norman on the wing you couldn't wish for a better triangular threesome in football. It was terrific.'

Jimmy McAlinden was part of the Belfast Celtic team that dominated the Irish League under Elisha Scott's direction. He missed out on an Irish Cup medal in 1937 because of injury. A year later he scored in Celtic's 2–1 defeat of Bangor. And he would also win medals in the 1941 and 1944 Cup finals.

McAlinden never hid his ambition to try full-time professional football in the Football League but had to be patient until the opportunity came his way in 1938.

'There had been talk in the papers for a couple of months about Norman Kernaghan and myself going to teams like Huddersfield and Tottenham Hotspur and I was hoping that something would materialise. Then, in early December 1938, Portsmouth came in for me and in a matter of a couple of weeks I was over there. It was a huge change which I never regretted. It was a wonderful life and if I had my life to live over I would do the same again.

'Portsmouth put a great deal of faith – and money – in me and it was justified. We won the FA Cup in 1939 so it was money well spent. Playing at Wembley is something one would not forget. Lots of people have scored hat-tricks against Linfield, but not too many have FA Cup medals.'

At the outbreak of war, the Portsmouth players had their contracts terminated and McAlinden rejoined Belfast Celtic. Before going back to Portsmouth after the war, McAlinden spent a season with Shamrock Rovers in Dublin. He subsequently moved on to play for Stoke City and then joined Southend on 5 October 1948 for £6,000.

McAlinden was capped four times for Ireland and went on a post-war tour to Spain and Portugal with the Republic of Ireland. When he retired from playing football, Jimmy Mac, as he was known, managed at Glenavon, Distillery and Drogheda.

Kevin McAlinden

Kevin McAlinden was a member of the bookmaking family which had long associations with Belfast Celtic. It was inevitable that he would join the club where he succeeded Tommy Breen in the first team in 1936 after winning several trophies for the second team. A leg injury sidelined Kevin in 1941 and he was displaced by Breen, who had returned from Manchester and, later, Hugh Kelly who was signed from Glenavon.

McAlinden moved to Coleraine during the 1947–8 season where, ironically, he played in the 3–2 Irish Cup semi-final defeat of Celtic. He returned to Paradise as first-choice goalkeeper for Celtic's last season. In the lead-up to the Boxing Day match against Linfield in 1948, McAlinden received hate mail warning him not to come to Windsor Park. He did play and was one of those attacked at the end of the game by a section of Linfield supporters. He was out of football for a couple of months but returned for the close of the season and was a member of the party which travelled to the US in April 1949.

Kevin won an amatuer international cap against England in 1947 and was selected for the Great Britain Olympic squad. He also represented both the Irish League and the League of Ireland when he played with Dundalk and Shelbourne.

Gerry McAloon

Gerry McAloon was in the latter part of his career when he joined Belfast Celtic from Glasgow Celtic. He had played in the forward line with Brentford before returning to Glasgow at the outbreak of the war. The *Irish News* reported his transfer to Belfast on Thursday, 19 August 1948: 'Gerry McAloon, Glasgow Celtic inside-forward transferred to Belfast Celtic for an undisclosed fee – assumed to be substantial. McAloon is a commercial traveller in Northern Ireland. Last season he travelled between Northern Ireland and Scotland via air to play for Celtic.'

Paddy McArdle

Paddy McArdle played in the forward line for Belfast Celtic and readily stepped into action for the first team when injury forced Jimmy McAlinden to drop out of selection for the 1937 Irish Cup final against Linfield. Celtic won 3–0 thanks to a Jimmy Turnbull hat-trick.

Bobby McAuley

Bobby McAuley's career at Belfast Celtic proved not to be a very happy one. The club was near his home in the Falls district and he eventually signed for them after Elisha Scott made several attempts to get him to Celtic Park from Distillery. In one of these, the Distillery manager had to order him out of Scott's office where McAuley was being 'interviewed'.

The relationship with the club, and Scott, turned sour when McAuley was trying to break through to the first team. 'We had a game at Bangor and with 15 minutes to go to kick-off, Celtic forward Liam O'Neill had not turned up. I was the reserve player and Scott told me to get changed. Just as we were about to go out on to the field, O'Neill arrived. He had been drinking. Scott was angry with him and tore strips off him. I couldn't believe when he told me that O'Neill was to play and I had to get changed again. It was so humiliating. I took the jersey off, threw it at Scott, got dressed and walked out. I never went back.'

McAuley made history by captaining junior side Dundela to a historic Irish Cup win over Glenavon in 1955.

Pat McAuley

Pat McAuley played at centre-forward during the early years of Belfast Celtic. He scored eight goals in Celtic's first Championship-winning season 1899–1900 and had the honour of being the first player from the club to win an international cap – against Scotland in 1900.

Sean McCann

Sean McCann grew up in Lurgan where he played Gaelic football with Hugh Kelly, who invited him along to Celtic Park for a goalkeeping trial. McCann spent two seasons at Paradise before moving to Ballymena United where he had been guaranteed first team football. He preferred to remain as an amateur in order to continue his involvement in swimming and water polo, and turned down Celtic's offer to turn professional even though he was promised a place on the US tour of 1949.

After his time with Ballymena, McCann played for Glenavon before ending his career as a professional with Portadown. He retired from football at the age of 27.

Sean McCarthy

Sean McCarthy established his reputation as a goalscorer at Cork United. Before moving to Celtic Park he was the League of Ireland's leading marksman on three consecutive seasons and it was hardly a surprise that word of his exploits reached Belfast. McCarthy, who succeeded former Celtic centre-forward Jimmy Turnbull at United, played as a full-time professional. The offer of higher wages lured him to Paradise in 1945 and he stayed until 1947. During that time he notched up 56 goals in his first season in the Regional League as well as winning a Gold Cup medal. He represented the League against the Combined Services in September 1945 and played in the 1946 Victory International against England.

McCarthy returned to Cork halfway through the 1946-7 season.

Keiller McCullough

Keiller McCullough came from Larne and joined Belfast Celtic in 1927. He had come through the ranks of the Intermediate League side, Newington Rangers, where his presence was made known to manager Austin Donnelly. He made such an impression during his first months at the club that the official programme of Belfast Celtic – 'The Celt' – profiled him in the 3 September 1927 issue. Ironically, that afternoon Celtic were playing Larne, who lined out a player at left-back called Fulton.

'The Celt' wrote of McCullough: 'He came, saw and conquered. It was a case of love at first sight. Twenty minutes' play of brilliant constructive football convinced the Celtic following that the newcomer was a player of exceptional promise.'

The skilful McCullough was praised for the way in which he had coped since his arrival at such a big club. 'McCullough has made good, but his success has not upset his mental equilibrium and he is content to stroll along at an easy pace picking up tricks and perfecting his football education in the premier school of Irish football, coached by two such experienced teachers as Hamill and Ferris.'

McCullough became an integral part of the Belfast Celtic forward line before transferring to Manchester City in November 1935. He won five international caps between 1935 and 1937.

Kevin McGarry

Kevin McGarry played as an amateur for Belfast Celtic in the 1940s and later moved to Cliftonville. McGarry, an inside-forward, won fifteen amateur and three international caps. He was also a member of the Great Britain Olympic squad and represented the Irish League on numerous occasions.

McGarry, who trained as a doctor, worked as a general practitioner in west Belfast.

Artie McGivern

Arthur McGivern belonged to the Belfast Celtic era of the 1930s. He played at outside-left for the Celtic Seconds team that won all the Intermediate League competitions in season 1934-5. McGivern scored in the 4–2 defeat by Linfield in the final of the County Antrim Shield that same year. McGivern also had the distinction of playing against Celtic's first team in the 1936 County Antrim Shield final. Again McGivern ended up on the losing side as Willie Donaghy scored the only goal of the game for the senior team. He was called up for first team duty on several occasions.

Jack McGrillen

Winger Jack McGrillen began his football career in the Falls League with Rosario before moving to Linfield where he was selected for the Ireland amateur international side against England in 1923–4. He also played at Clyde for a season and partnered Billy Gillepsie up front against Scotland at Parkhead in 1924. He won a second cap against Scotland in 1927.

Charlie McIlroy

Ballymena born Charlie McIlroy was 21 years old when he joined Belfast Celtic as an outside-left in the mid-1930s. He won all the major domestic honours at Paradise.

Syd McIlroy

Syd McIlroy came from Larne. He played at inside-left or on the wing.

Billy McMillan

Billy McMillan played at right-back for Belfast Celtic. He joined the club in 1932 and stayed there until its departure from the Irish League in 1949. He was a product of Charlie Murphy's very successful Celtic Seconds team and once he had established himself in the first team, he was rarely absent.

McMillan was part of the Celtic squad that successfully toured the US in 1949.

Apart from three appearances in the Victory Internationals of 1946, Carrickfergus-born McMillan never gained full recognition with Ireland or Northern Ireland. Ironically, he did represent the Republic of Ireland when it played two games against Portugal and Spain in June 1946.

Eddie McMorran

Linfield's loss proved to be Belfast Celtic's gain when Elisha Scott signed centre-forward Eddie McMorran from Larne. He had been with Linfield Swifts, but moved to Celtic Park on better terms and used his time with the Celts as a springboard to the Football League. He was top scorer in the 1946–7 Gold Cup tournament with 21 goals in 13 games. In the Regional League his 30 goals in 24 games confirmed the judgement of Manchester City who signed him in 1947. McMorran had spells with Barnsley and Doncaster United. He won the first of his 15 caps against England as a Belfast Celtic player.

Mick McWilliams

Mick McWilliams played in defence, as an amateur, for Belfast Celtic and Linfield. He was studying to become a teacher in 1937 when he was asked to go along to Celtic Park for a trial. He lived in Ballyclare, outside Belfast, and knew very little about the history of the club. He stayed with them for five years before moving to Windsor Park.

'I wanted first-team football and there was no guarantee of that with Celtic, who had signed Joe Douglas. After speaking to Tommy Breen who was already at Linfield, I went along for a trial and stayed with them for five years.'

Mick McWilliams recalls that the atmosphere at Linfield seemed to be much friendlier than at Celtic Park. 'Being a Catholic at Linfield didn't appear to mean anything that I can remember. Tommy Breen was there and then Davy Walsh came up from the south.

'When we won the Irish Cup in 1945 and 1946 there wasn't an official team photograph with the trophy. Tommy Breen remarked that it might have something to do with the inner-thinking of some of the Linfield people. There were three Catholics on the team, but no photograph. It does seem strange.'

McWilliams, who returned to Celtic Park several times to play against his old team, is adamant that whatever animosity existed between the supporters, who were segregated, never extended to the teams. 'I suppose the bigotry was as rampant then as it is today, but we didn't worry about it that much.

'At Grosvenor Park where Distillery played, it was a tight ground with the crowd right on top of you. Once when I was playing for Celtic, I was taking a throw-in and someone shouted, "You black-haired Fenian, you'll be the next f***ing Pope." All you could do was laugh at it.'

Mick McWilliams joined Ballymena United from Linfield, but his career at the Showgrounds was cut short by a knee injury. He was a spectator at Windsor Park on Boxing Day 1948.

'When we played each other, it was always a tight game, but that was the worst thing I had ever witnessed. People knew that something different was going to happen, possibly because of what had happened in the previous game. The threats were coming from the Blues supporters that certain things would be done, that it wouldn't be an easy walkover for Celtic. I was disgusted by the whole thing.'

And McWilliams was not that surprised when Belfast Celtic withdrew from the Irish League. 'I knew the club were going to come out of football. John Fitzpatrick was a director of the club and I was friendly with his sons, Brendan and Mick. They told me that once Celtic were out, it would be a long time before they came back.'

Bertie Mehaffey

Bertie Mehaffey was goalkeeper with Celtic when it clinched the Irish League Championship in 1915. During the war years when Celtic played as a junior side, he was succeeded by his first cousin Elisha Scott. The infamous, abandoned Irish Cup replay between Celtic and Glentoran in March 1920 featured two goalkeepers called Mehaffey – Bertie of Celtic and his brother John who was playing for the Glens.

Sammy Moore

Sammy Moore joined Belfast Celtic from junior football in Derry on its return to the Irish League in 1924 and played in the half-back line with Eddie Inch and Billy Pollock. The following season he captained Celtic. Team manager, Austin Donnelly, once said of the popular Derry man, 'When an amateur, he was a genuine amateur; he would not even accept his tram fares.' Moore, who was quiet and unassuming off the field, would undergo a personality change when he was playing. He refused countless inducements to leave Celtic Park.

Gerry Murray

Gerry Murray was born in Belfast and joined Celtic in the 1930s following a spell at Linfield. He was promoted from the second team and slotted into the defence alongside Harry Walker and 'Scotty' Walker when Keiller McCullough moved to Manchester City. He later moved on to Glentoran where he became team captain.

Peter O'Connor

Centre-forward Peter O'Connor earned a unique place in football's history books when he scored 11 goals in Belfast Celtic's 13–0 defeat of Glenavon at Celtic Park in January 1941. This individual scoring record has never been equalled in a League game, in Ireland or Britain, and it may stay that way.

O'Connor came from Ballymoney in County Antrim and graduated from junior football to Celtic Park in 1932 after a short, unsuccessful period at Windsor Park. He spent several seasons as captain of Belfast Celtic Seconds before breaking through to the first team in season 1938–9 when Jimmy Turnbull was injured. O'Connor made his own mark on the game that year by scoring over 50 goals.

His collection of trophies included six Championship medals and four Irish Cup medals. When he retired from playing, he became Glasgow Celtic's scout in Ireland and sent them Charlie Tully, Sean Fallon and Bertie Peacock.

Peter O'Connor emigrated to America during the 1950s and died at his home in Rochester, New York in 1994.

Harry O'Neill

Harry O'Neill played Gaelic football for Antrim before trying his luck with Belfast Celtic. He played with the second team and got a couple of games with the Firsts.

Liam O'Neill

Liam O'Neill was one of a batch of players that came to Belfast Celtic from Cork. He played in the forward line and was a consistent scorer for the club.

Malachy O'Neill

Malachy O'Neill played mostly for the second team.

Billy Pollock

Billy Pollock graduated from the minor leagues in Belfast and signed for Celtic prior to its return in 1924. His favourite position was at either right or left half and once Pollock won his place in the team his total commitment made him difficult to displace.

Reggie Simpson

Reggie Simpson was the older brother of Northern Ireland centre-forward Billy who played at Linfield and Glasgow Rangers. Reggie, a left-back, was a regular first team player and was part of the squad which travelled to America in 1949.

Andy Smith

Andy Smith played at centre-forward for Celtic on its return to football in 1924. He became a Celtic Park hero because of his versatility – he could switch to half-back. Andy was the club's top scorer in 1924–5 with 18 goals.

James Smith

James Smith started the 1925 season as first-choice goalkeeper. At six feet and half an inch, he was the tallest player on the team. He had played with Oldpark and Dunmurry before being spotted by Celtic.

Len Townsend

Len Townsend came to Northern Ireland in 1943 from Brentford as a replacement for Paddy Bonnar who had suffered a long-term injury. Townsend's impact was immediate. He scored eight goals in Celtic's successful run through the County Antrim Shield competition. Townsend also played in the Irish Cup final and set up the pass for Bill Hollinger to score the only goal against Glentoran in the 1943 final.

Oscar Traynor

Oscar Traynor played at Paradise before the First World War. He was a giant of a goalkeeper who stood out above the rest of the team. He was a member of the side that won the inaugural Gold Cup in 1912 and travelled with the club on its tour to Bohemia. Traynor moved into politics afterwards. He fought in the 1916 Easter Rebellion and was elected to the Dáil in 1925. Traynor served as Minister of Defence in the Free State government and was president of the Football Association of Ireland for 15 years. He died in 1963.

Tommy Tucker

Tommy Tucker was an inside-left who played mostly for Belfast Celtic Seconds.

Charlie Tully

Charlie Tully proved to be one of Belfast Celtic's great discoveries and before he transferred to Glasgow Celtic in 1948 for a fee of £8,000, he thrilled football fans throughout Ireland with his wizardry and tantalising skills. 'Cheeky' Charlie was born in the Falls district in 1924 and signed for Belfast Celtic as a schoolboy. He went on loan to Cliftonville for a short period before establishing himself in the Celtic first team.

He won ten international caps following his transfer to Glasgow Celtic.

Jimmy Turnbull

Jimmy Turnbull came from Gateshead in the north east of England. He had played with Barnsley and in North America before making a major impact at Cork in 1935–6, where he scored 37 of the club's 61 goals to help it to third place in the League of Ireland Championship.

Elisha Scott tempted Turnbull to come to Belfast and the Geordie continued his prowess in front of goal where he established a club record of 82 League and Cup goals in 1936–7.

The following season Turnbull's tally was 62 goals as Belfast Celtic retained the Irish League Championship.

When a foot injury sidelined Turnbull, Peter O'Connor took over to lead the Celtic attack for the 1938–9 season. Turnbull returned to Cork with many special memories, including a Cup final hat-trick against Linfield, an individual scoring record of seven goals in a game against Cliftonville and a special place in Belfast Celtic's history. When Turnbull retired, he concentrated on running his pub which was aptly named 'The Centre Forward'.

Jackie Vernon

John Joseph Vernon was born in Jocelyn Avenue, Belfast in 1919 and when he left school to learn his trade in the family butchery business, he served his time in football's unofficial apprenticeship scheme with Spearmint FC – a summer League team – and then Dundela.

Vernon, a rugged centre-half, rejected an approach by Liverpool and chose instead to sign on at Celtic Park where his education continued in the second team. Promotion to first-team duty came when Scott Walker returned to Scotland at the outbreak of the war and a place was made in the defence for 20-year-old Vernon. He accepted the chance with relish as Belfast Celtic collected their fifth successive League Championship.

International honours followed in 1946 with three Victory caps and, as Vernon's reputation continued to spread, he won the first of 17 full international caps against England in 1947.

Following Celtic's 3–2 defeat by Linfield at Paradise, on Saturday, 8 February 1947, a bid of £9,500 from West Bromwich Albion was accepted for Vernon. Glasgow Celtic could have paid a lot less. Parkhead manager Jimmy McCrory thought Belfast Celtic's valuation of £8,000 was too high.

Jackie Vernon played for the Great Britain team against the Rest of the World at Hampden Park in 1947 and captained a Rest of Britain team against Wales in an anniversary match at Ninian Park.

He returned to the Irish League as player–manager of Crusaders, the club that replaced Belfast Celtic, in 1952.

Jackie Vernon died suddenly on 24 August 1981, aged 62.

Harry Walker

Harry Walker was first signed by Mickey Hamill in 1929 as a 17-year-old when Belfast Celtic Seconds were playing in the Alliance League. But the teenage Walker was unable to break into the side and moved on to Glentoran later that season.

Glentoran did not recognise Walker's potential and he had periods with Bradbury United, Linfield, Ards and Crusaders before he eventually returned to Paradise. His first team debut was against Derry City, on Christmas Day 1932.

Harry was born into a working-class Protestant environment in the Bloomfield Road, east Belfast. His father Jack had been a professional footballer and had also played at Celtic Park. Walker was always aware of the intense rivalry between Belfast's biggest clubs.

'Results against Linfield were always important. I remember Celtic winning one encounter by eight goals to one, but early in my career we lost a cup match 7–0. The following Saturday when we met again, Jackie Donnelly scored for the Blues within 30 seconds. But Celtic fought back to win, thanks to a Davy Martin hat-trick.

'While the supporters had their differences and the occasional fights, generally both teams were very friendly with each other. No matter how much we kicked at each other, once the match ended we'd go and have a yarn and a bottle of Guinness.'

Harry Walker scored the first goal in the 1948 Boxing Day game and had to fight with the mob that invaded the pitch at full-time to get his goalkeeper Kevin McAlinden to safety.

'When the whistle went we started shaking hands and then I saw the crowds coming over from the Spion Kop and going for Kevin. The police did not help very much. I caught one spectator who kicked me on the knee and all that a policeman said to him was "Go away and behave yourself."'

Walker was one of the first players to know that Belfast Celtic were to withdraw from the Irish League though he was never convinced that the Boxing Day incident was the real reason.

'I think the Jimmy Jones episode was the excuse that some of the board had been looking for. There had been rumours of some kind of dispute in the boardroom at the time which neither lot seemed to want to settle. There's no doubt that Belfast Celtic could have played on until 1969 when the civil troubles began but it would have been impossible to continue after that.'

It remains a mystery why Harry Walker, who played for Ireland at junior level, was never awarded a senior cap. Arsenal and Fulham had expressed an interest in signing Walker but the transfers were never finalised.

After his 17 years at Belfast Celtic, Walker played and coached at Ards and later moved on to manage Glenavon and Portadown.

Jap Walker

John 'Jap' Walker was the only Scotsman ever to play for Ireland. His parents had moved to Glagow for a few years and John was born there. The family returned to Belfast where John grew up. He played for Belfast Celtic and was transferred to First Division Bury in 1910. After he had won an international cap against Scotland in 1911, it was discovered that he had not been born in Ireland and he was never selected again.

Scotty Walker

John 'Scotty' Walker joined Belfast Celtic in the 1930s. He played in the half-back line with Harry Walker, Keiller McCullough and Gerry Murray. At the outbreak of the war he returned to his native Scotland.

TWELVE

FACTS & FIGURES

HONOURS: BELFAST CELTIC

Irish League Championship (14)
1899–1900, 1914–5, 1919–20, 1925–6, 1926–7, 1927–8,
1928–9, 1932–3, 1935–6, 1936–7, 1937–8, 1938–9,
1939–40, 1947–8.

Irish Cup (8)
1917–8, 1925–6, 1936–7, 1937–8, 1940–1, 1942–3,
1943–4, 1946–7.

Gold Cup (7)
1911–2, 1925–6, 1934–5, 1938–9, 1939–40, 1946–7,
1947–8.

City Cup (10)
1905–6, 1906–7, 1925–6, 1927–8, 1929–30, 1930–1,
1932–3, 1939–40, 1947–8, 1948–9.

County Antrim Shield (8)
1894–5, 1909–10, 1926–7, 1935–6, 1936–7, 1938–9,
1942–3, 1944–5.

Steel and Sons Cup (5)
1912–3, 1916–7, 1917–8, 1934-5, 1935–6.

Regional League Champions (4)
1940–1, 1941–2, 1942–3, 1946–7.

Regional Gold Cup (3)
1940–1,   1943–4,   1945–6.

Intermediate League Champions (7)
1916–7,   1917–8,   1931–2,   1933–4,   1934–5, 1935–6,
1936–7.

Intermediate Cup (5)
1913–4,   1934–5,   1935–6,   1936–7,   1939–40.

IRISH LEAGUE TABLES

Season 1896–7

	P	W	D	L	F	A	Pts
Glentoran	10	9	1	1	24	10	19
Cliftonville	10	4	3	3	22	20	11
Linfield	10	4	3	3	34	24	11
Distillery	10	3	3	4	17	23	9
North Staffordshire	10	2	4	4	17	23	8
Belfast Celtic	*10*	*1*	*2*	*7*	*11*	*25*	*4*

Season 1897–8

	P	W	D	L	F	A	Pts
Linfield	10	8	1	1	22	10	17
Cliftonville	10	6	1	3	23	17	13
Glentoran	10	6	1	3	31	12	13
Belfast Celtic	*10*	*3*	*1*	*6*	*15*	*19*	*7*
Distillery	10	2	1	7	13	28	5
North Staffordshire	10	2	1	7	13	31	5

Season 1898–9

	P	W	D	L	F	A	Pts
Distillery	10	7	1	2	23	17	15
Linfield	10	7	1	2	21	8	15
Cliftonville	10	6	0	4	19	12	12
Glentoran	10	6	0	4	17	12	12
Belfast Celtic	*10*	*2*	*2*	*6*	*15*	*25*	*6*

	P	W	D	L	F	A	Pts
North Staffordshire	10	0	0	10	11	32	0

Season 1899–1900

	P	W	D	L	F	A	Pts
Belfast Celtic	*8*	*5*	*1*	*2*	*18*	*11*	*11*
Linfield	8	3	4	1	16	10	10
Cliftonville	8	3	3	2	16	16	9
Distillery	8	2	4	2	11	13	8
Glentoran	8	0	2	6	7	18	2

Season 1900–1

	P	W	D	L	F	A	Pts
Distillery	10	7	2	1	33	10	16
Glentoran	10	7	1	2	24	13	15
Belfast Celtic	*10*	*4*	*2*	*4*	*13*	*13*	*10*
Cliftonville	10	3	4	3	17	18	10
Linfield	10	3	2	5	10	12	8
Derry Celtic	10	0	1	9	12	43	1

Season 1901–2

	P	W	D	L	F	A	Pts
Linfield	14	12	0	2	38	10	24
Glentoran	14	10	1	3	39	19	21
Distillery	14	8	3	3	38	20	19
Cliftonville	14	7	2	5	24	14	16
Belfast Celtic	*14*	*4*	*4*	*6*	*22*	*24*	*12*
Derry Celtic	14	5	2	7	23	26	12
Ulster	14	2	3	9	22	44	7
St. Columb's Court	14	0	1	13	13	62	1

Season 1902–3

	P	W	D	L	F	A	Pts
Distillery	14	9	2	3	34	20	20
Linfield	14	8	3	3	36	16	19
Glentoran	14	7	3	4	30	18	17
Belfast Celtic	*14*	*7*	*2*	*5*	*35*	*23*	*16*
Cliftonville	14	5	3	6	17	21	11*
Derry Celtic	14	4	4	6	27	31	12

| Bohemians | 14 | 3 | 3 | 8 | 22 | 26 | 9 |
| Ulster | 14 | 3 | 0 | 11 | 13 | 51 | 6 |

*Cliftonville had two points deducted

Season 1903–4

	P	W	D	L	F	A	Pts
Linfield	14	12	2	0	47	9	26
Distillery	14	8	4	2	35	13	20
Glentoran	14	7	6	1	20	9	20
Belfast Celtic	*14*	*5*	*2*	*7*	*27*	*20*	*12*
Cliftonville	14	5	2	7	22	29	12
Bohemians	14	4	3	7	24	33	11
Derry Celtic	14	3	2	9	17	26	8
Scott Borderers	14	1	1	12	11	64	3

Season 1904–5

	P	W	D	L	F	A	Pts
Glentoran	14	9	3	2	22	12	21*
Belfast Celtic	*14*	*9*	*3*	*2*	*21*	*10*	*21*
Linfield	14	6	4	4	18	12	16
Distillery	14	6	3	5	16	11	15
Cliftonville	14	6	1	7	17	17	13
Shelbourne	14	5	3	6	15	17	13
Derry Celtic	14	1	5	8	12	31	7
Bohemians	14	2	2	10	15	26	6

*Glentoran won the play-off for the Championship.

Season 1905–6

	P	W	D	L	F	A	Pts
Cliftonville	14	7	5	2	19	8	19
Distillery	14	8	3	3	20	13	19
Linfield	14	7	3	4	21	14	17
Belfast Celtic	*14*	*6*	*3*	*5*	*20*	*18*	*15*
Bohemians	14	5	2	7	17	20	12
Shelbourne	14	5	2	7	16	18	12
Derry Celtic	14	4	3	7	13	22	11
Glentoran	14	2	3	9	13	26	7

Season 1906–7

	P	W	D	L	F	A	Pts
Linfield	14	10	3	1	30	9	23
Shelbourne	14	8	3	3	27	21	19
Distillery	14	6	4	4	27	22	16
Cliftonville	14	4	6	4	18	16	14
Bohemians	14	4	5	5	19	22	13
Belfast Celtic	*14*	*4*	*3*	*7*	*18*	*25*	*11*
Glentoran	14	2	5	7	18	25	9
Derry Celtic	14	2	3	9	11	28	7

Season 1907–8

	P	W	D	L	F	A	Pts
Linfield	14	10	2	2	31	15	22
Glentoran	14	7	3	4	27	23	17
Cliftonville	14	6	5	3	22	16	17
Distillery	14	6	2	6	21	21	14
Shelbourne	14	6	2	6	22	17	14
Belfast Celtic	*14*	*5*	*1*	*7*	*20*	*20*	*11*
Derry Celtic	14	4	1	9	16	30	9
Bohemians	14	2	2	9	13	30	6

Season 1908–9

	P	W	D	L	F	A	Pts
Linfield	14	10	1	3	27	13	21
Glentoran	14	8	3	3	29	22	19
Shelbourne	14	7	1	6	20	20	15
Distillery	14	6	1	7	22	19	13
Bohemians	14	6	1	6	28	29	13
Belfast Celtic	*14*	*5*	*2*	*7*	*26*	*33*	*12*
Cliftonville	14	4	2	7	17	19	10
Derry Celtic	14	4	0	10	12	26	8

Season 1909-10

	P	W	D	L	F	A	Pts
Cliftonville	14	8	4	2	25	14	20
Belfast Celtic	*14*	*9*	*0*	*5*	*25*	*13*	*18*
Linfield	14	5	5	4	19	20	15

	P	W	D	L	F	A	Pts
Distillery	14	5	3	6	14	13	13
Derry Celtic	14	4	5	5	19	21	13
Bohemians	14	4	3	7	20	31	11
Glentoran	14	5	1	8	23	23	11
Shelbourne	14	2	7	5	15	24	11

Season 1910–1

	P	W	D	L	F	A	Pts
Linfield	14	9	4	1	29	11	22
Glentoran	14	10	2	2	39	12	22
Belfast Celtic	*14*	*5*	*5*	*4*	*21*	*19*	*15*
Cliftonville	14	5	4	5	16	22	14
Derry Celtic	14	5	4	5	21	29	14
Shelbourne	14	3	4	7	15	31	10
Distillery	14	2	5	7	13	19	9
Bohemians	14	1	4	9	14	25	6

Season 1911–2

	P	W	D	L	F	A	Pts
Glentoran	14	10	3	1	41	11	23
Distillery	14	9	3	2	32	14	21
Belfast Celtic	*14*	*7*	*6*	*1*	*21*	*11*	*20*
Linfield	14	6	4	4	25	16	16
Derry Celtic	14	5	1	8	16	30	11
Shelbourne	14	2	4	8	10	28	8
Cliftonville	14	3	1	10	14	36	7
Glenavon	14	2	2	10	17	30	6

Season 1912–3

	P	W	D	L	F	A	Pts
Glentoran	18	12	2	4	35	16	26
Distillery	18	11	2	5	34	17	24
Linfield	18	9	5	4	29	23	23
Glenavon	18	9	2	7	25	17	20
Cliftonville	18	8	3	7	23	23	19
Bohemians	18	8	2	8	31	29	18
Belfast Celtic	*18*	*7*	*4*	*7*	*24*	*26*	*18*
Shelbourne	18	7	4	7	20	23	18

	P	W	D	L	F	A	Pts
Derry Celtic	18	3	3	12	18	39	9
Tritonville	18	2	1	15	27	55	5

SEASON 1913-4

	P	W	D	L	F	A	Pts
Linfield	14	11	2	1	32	13	24
Glentoran	14	8	3	3	32	18	19
Belfast Celtic	*14*	*8*	*1*	*5*	*19*	*18*	*17*
Distillery	14	6	4	4	14	12	16
Shelbourne	14	6	2	6	16	10	14
Glenavon	14	4	2	8	12	23	10
Bohemians	14	2	2	10	19	36	6
Cliftonville	14	3	0	11	15	29	6

SEASON 1914–5

	P	W	D	L	F	A	Pts
Belfast Celtic	*14*	*10*	*3*	*1*	*24*	*7*	*23*
Glentoran	14	9	3	2	27	11	21
Linfield	14	6	5	3	27	18	17
Distillery	14	7	1	6	23	16	15
Shelbourne	14	6	3	5	17	13	15
Glenavon	14	3	5	6	24	27	11
Cliftonville	14	4	1	9	14	29	9
Bohemians	14	0	1	13	10	45	1

The Irish League Championship was suspended during the First World War.

SEASON 1919–20

	P	W	D	L	F	A	Pts
Belfast Celtic	*14*	*10*	*3*	*1*	*27*	*6*	*23*
Distillery	14	7	6	1	26	9	20
Glentoran	14	8	3	3	29	10	19
Shelbourne	14	3	7	4	16	21	13
Linfield	14	4	4	6	8	11	12
Glenavon	14	3	4	7	21	28	10
Cliftonville	14	2	5	7	13	24	9
Bohemians	14	2	2	10	7	38	6

Belfast Celtic withdrew until 1924 due to civil unrest.

Season 1924–5

	P	W	D	L	F	A	Pts
Glentoran	22	17	3	2	53	18	37
Queens Island	22	13	6	3	48	23	32
Belfast Celtic	*22*	*11*	*5*	*6*	*36*	*31*	*27*
Portadown	22	10	5	7	41	35	25
Glenavon	22	11	2	9	45	36	24
Linfield	22	10	2	10	34	31	22
Ards	22	7	4	11	39	41	18
Larne	22	7	4	11	30	47	18
Barn United	22	6	4	12	29	40	16
Cliftonville	22	6	4	12	21	32	16
Distillery	22	6	4	12	31	40	16
Newry Town	22	5	3	14	34	67	13

Season 1925–6

	P	W	D	L	F	A	Pts
Belfast Celtic	*22*	*16*	*1*	*5*	*52*	*38*	*33*
Glentoran	22	13	4	5	52	30	30
Larne	22	11	5	6	49	33	27
Ards	22	11	4	7	56	43	26
Distillery	22	10	5	7	37	35	25
Queens Island	22	9	5	8	42	37	23
Glenavon	22	10	3	9	35	37	23
Linfield	22	8	5	9	47	50	21
Portadown	22	7	7	8	43	41	21
Newry Town	22	5	5	12	33	51	15
Cliftonville	22	4	6	12	29	37	14
Bangor	22	2	2	18	25	64	6

Season 1926–7

	P	W	D	L	F	A	Pts
Belfast Celtic	*22*	*15*	*7*	*0*	*66*	*26*	*37*
Queens Island	22	12	6	4	46	34	30
Distillery	22	12	5	5	56	36	29
Glentoran	22	11	5	6	56	47	27
Ards	22	9	7	6	42	42	25
Larne	22	10	4	8	55	48	24

	P	W	D	L	F	A	Pts
Linfield	22	8	6	8	41	35	22
Portadown	22	7	4	11	50	48	18
Cliftonville	22	7	3	12	32	40	17
Newry Town	22	6	5	11	39	48	17
Glenavon	22	4	3	15	33	57	11
Barn United	22	2	3	17	35	89	7

SEASON 1927–8

	P	W	D	L	F	A	Pts
Belfast Celtic	*26*	*20*	*5*	*1*	*101*	*35*	*45*
Linfield	26	18	5	3	88	34	41
Newry Town	26	13	7	6	55	30	33
Larne	26	13	4	9	63	55	30
Glentoran	26	12	5	9	63	65	29
Coleraine	26	11	5	10	57	60	27
Distillery	26	9	7	10	45	44	25
Bangor	26	9	5	12	57	69	23
Glenavon	26	9	5	12	63	69	23
Portadown	26	10	3	14	46	69	17
Barn United	26	5	4	17	38	91	14
Cliftonville	26	5	3	18	29	72	13

SEASON 1928–9

	P	W	D	L	F	A	Pts
Belfast Celtic	*26*	*22*	*4*	*0*	*116*	*23*	*48*
Linfield	26	19	1	6	88	44	39
Glentoran	26	15	3	8	85	59	33
Distillery	26	15	2	9	71	58	32
Coleraine	26	13	4	9	63	53	30
Ballymena United	26	10	8	8	63	55	28
Bangor	26	10	6	10	49	52	26
Glenavon	26	8	8	10	61	63	24
Ards	26	9	5	12	55	64	23
Newry Town	26	9	4	13	46	58	22
Portadown	26	10	2	14	52	76	22
Larne	26	8	4	14	49	75	20
Cliftonville	26	3	4	19	32	73	10
Queens Island	26	2	3	21	53	130	7

Season 1929–30

	P	W	D	L	F	A	Pts
Linfield	26	19	4	3	92	44	42
Glentoran	26	16	4	6	79	53	36
Coleraine	26	14	4	8	66	46	32
Belfast Celtic	*26*	*13*	*4*	*9*	*68*	*57*	*30*
Bangor	26	12	5	9	60	57	29
Ballymena United	26	13	3	10	65	46	29
Derry City	26	12	5	9	52	55	29
Distillery	26	12	3	11	65	62	27
Glenavon	26	12	3	11	70	63	27
Portadown	26	7	7	12	68	90	21
Newry Town	26	9	1	16	51	66	19
Ards	26	6	6	14	47	77	18
Larne	26	5	3	18	47	77	13
Cliftonville	26	5	2	19	40	77	12

Season 1930–1

	P	W	D	L	F	A	Pts
Glentoran	26	22	3	1	96	39	47
Linfield	26	16	6	4	73	42	38
Belfast Celtic	*26*	*16*	*4*	*6*	*75*	*52*	*36*
Distillery	26	15	4	7	82	46	34
Ballymena United	26	13	5	8	75	51	31
Ards	26	11	5	10	68	69	27
Derry City	26	10	4	12	50	61	24
Cliftonville	26	11	2	13	54	70	24
Portadown	26	7	5	14	63	73	19
Bangor	26	7	5	14	62	75	19
Glenavon	26	8	3	15	47	76	19
Coleraine	26	6	6	14	48	56	18
Larne	26	6	6	14	44	73	18
Newry Town	26	4	2	20	54	100	10

Season 1931–2

	P	W	D	L	F	A	Pts
Linfield	26	20	3	3	78	32	43
Derry City	26	16	6	4	61	30	38
Belfast Celtic	*26*	*14*	*5*	*7*	*55*	*36*	*33*
Coleraine	26	13	6	7	67	54	32
Glentoran	26	12	7	7	73	54	31
Cliftonville	26	11	5	10	59	55	27
Ballymena United	26	11	5	10	65	41	27
Distillery	26	8	7	11	57	68	23
Portadown	26	8	6	12	54	63	22
Newry Town	26	9	4	13	43	53	22
Larne	26	6	7	13	47	85	19
Ards	26	7	4	15	52	81	18
Glenavon	26	6	5	15	42	74	17
Bangor	26	3	6	17	41	68	12

Season 1932–3

	P	W	D	L	F	A	Pts
Belfast Celtic	*26*	*19*	*3*	*4*	*81*	*34*	*41*
Distillery	26	18	3	5	75	47	39
Linfield	26	17	4	5	83	34	38
Derry City	26	16	1	9	59	39	33
Glentoran	26	14	4	8	74	61	32
Bangor	26	13	2	11	60	56	28
Coleraine	26	11	5	10	69	50	27
Ballymena United	26	11	4	11	56	58	26
Glenavon	26	7	4	15	56	59	18
Portadown	26	8	2	16	37	72	18
Larne	26	8	1	17	55	88	17
Ards	26	6	5	15	51	83	17
Cliftonville	26	5	6	15	54	74	16
Newry Town	26	5	4	17	47	102	14

Season 1933–4

	P	W	D	L	F	A	Pts
Linfield	26	22	2	2	88	21	46
Belfast Celtic	*26*	*17*	*3*	*6*	*74*	*42*	*37*

	P	W	D	L	F	A	Pts
Glentoran	26	16	3	7	59	36	35
Distillery	26	14	3	9	61	41	31
Ballymena United	26	12	6	8	59	46	30
Ards	26	11	5	10	47	46	27
Portadown	26	10	5	11	41	52	25
Glenavon	26	10	4	12	45	54	24
Derry City	26	8	7	11	37	38	23
Cliftonville	26	11	0	15	50	78	22
Bangor	26	7	4	15	43	58	18
Coleraine	26	7	3	16	40	61	17
Newry Town	26	5	6	15	37	71	16
Larne	26	4	5	17	37	74	13

Season 1934–5

	P	W	D	L	F	A	Pts
Linfield	26	21	4	1	76	19	46
Derry City	26	18	4	4	64	32	40
Belfast Celtic	*26*	*17*	*3*	*6*	*96*	*36*	*37*
Glentoran	26	16	4	6	70	42	36
Portadown	26	14	5	7	56	38	33
Distillery	26	11	5	10	47	44	27
Larne	26	11	5	10	48	53	27
Glenavon	26	7	7	12	43	55	21
Ballymena United	26	7	5	14	48	65	19
Cliftonville	26	8	3	15	45	69	19
Newry Town	26	8	1	17	60	76	17
Coleraine	26	7	2	17	43	66	16
Ards	26	5	3	18	46	91	13
Bangor	26	3	7	16	39	95	13

Season 1935–6

	P	W	D	L	F	A	Pts
Belfast Celtic	*26*	*20*	*3*	*3*	*67*	*23*	*43*
Derry City	26	18	5	3	71	36	41
Linfield	26	17	4	5	72	28	38
Newry Town	26	14	5	7	80	50	33
Glentoran	26	12	3	11	57	50	27
Distillery	26	11	5	10	50	52	27

Larne	26	11	4	11	49	65	26
Portadown	26	9	5	12	53	58	23
Cliftonville	26	9	5	12	49	61	23
Ballymena United	26	7	5	14	41	59	19
Bangor	26	8	3	15	47	72	19
Glenavon	26	6	5	15	40	56	17
Coleraine	26	5	5	16	28	44	15
Ards	26	5	3	18	44	94	13

Season 1936–7

	P	W	D	L	F	A	Pts
Belfast Celtic	*26*	*20*	*4*	*2*	*86*	*21*	*44*
Derry City	26	20	3	3	84	36	43
Linfield	26	20	2	4	85	25	42
Portadown	26	14	4	8	49	38	32
Larne	26	13	2	11	63	57	28
Newry Town	26	12	3	11	59	48	27
Glentoran	26	11	3	12	65	65	25
Cliftonville	26	9	6	11	55	63	24
Glenavon	26	10	1	15	56	59	21
Bangor	26	8	3	15	40	80	19
Coleraine	26	7	5	14	25	60	19
Ards	26	8	2	16	42	73	18
Distillery	26	6	2	18	36	65	14
Ballymena United	26	3	2	21	33	88	8

Season 1937–8

	P	W	D	L	F	A	Pts
Belfast Celtic	*26*	*18*	*5*	*3*	*86*	*22*	*41**
Derry City	26	20	1	5	81	40	41
Portadown	26	16	5	5	67	32	37
Linfield	26	16	5	5	78	38	37
Ballymena United	26	14	5	7	72	55	33
Glentoran	26	15	2	9	64	57	32
Newry Town	26	10	6	10	63	49	26
Distillery	26	10	6	10	51	61	26
Ards	26	7	4	15	43	66	18
Glenavon	26	6	5	15	36	55	17

	P	W	D	L	F	A	Pts
Bangor	26	7	2	17	39	62	16
Larne	26	6	3	17	48	87	15
Coleraine	26	5	5	16	40	75	15
Cliftonville	26	2	6	18	27	86	10

*Belfast Celtic won the Championship following a play-off.

Season 1938–9

	P	W	D	L	F	A	Pts
Belfast Celtic	26	19	2	5	97	32	40
Ballymena United	26	15	5	6	63	54	35
Derry City	26	15	3	8	84	46	33
Portadown	26	15	3	8	84	56	33
Linfield	26	14	2	10	58	40	30
Glentoran	26	14	1	11	64	68	29
Glenavon	26	12	4	10	67	57	28
Ards	26	11	6	9	63	66	28
Newry Town	26	9	8	9	43	48	26
Distillery	26	9	4	13	53	56	22
Larne	26	8	4	14	45	74	20
Bangor	26	6	7	13	38	72	19
Cliftonville	26	5	2	19	38	81	12
Coleraine	26	3	3	20	40	87	9

Season 1939–40

	P	W	D	L	F	A	Pts
Belfast Celtic	26	20	5	1	91	18	45
Portadown	26	18	5	3	86	37	41
Glentoran	26	19	1	6	103	45	39
Ballymena United	26	15	4	7	82	52	34
Linfield	26	13	5	8	62	48	31
Derry City	26	14	2	10	73	46	30
Glenavon	26	13	3	10	69	68	29
Ards	26	11	2	13	52	69	24
Coleraine	26	10	2	14	45	70	22
Bangor	26	8	3	15	44	77	19
Distillery	26	6	3	17	53	70	15
Newry Town	26	5	5	16	32	86	15
Larne	26	4	5	17	36	83	13

| Cliftonville | 26 | 3 | 1 | 22 | 40 | 99 | 7 |

The Irish League Championship was suspended from season 1940-1; it resumed in season 1947–8. A regional League was organised in its place during those years.

Regional League 1940–1

	P	W	D	L	F	A	Pts
Belfast Celtic	27	19	4	4	104	32	42
Portadown	27	17	4	6	92	68	38
Glentoran	28	16	5	7	100	57	37
Linfield	27	14	4	9	68	52	32
Distillery	28	13	5	10	77	56	31
Derry City	28	8	3	17	47	90	19
Glenavon	27	6	4	17	40	95	16
Cliftonville	28	2	1	25	39	115	5

Portadown *v* Belfast Celtic and Glenavon *v* Linfield not played.

Regional League 1941–2

	P	W	D	L	F	A	Pts
Belfast Celtic	20	12	6	2	5	23	30
Linfield	20	11	7	2	64	38	29
Glentoran	20	11	3	6	59	37	25
Distillery	20	6	6	8	41	37	18
Derry City	20	3	5	12	23	73	11
Cliftonville	20	2	3	15	23	64	7

Regional League 1942–3

	P	W	D	L	F	A	Pts
Linfield	20	14	2	4	55	26	30
Belfast Celtic	20	13	3	4	5	2	29
Distillery	20	10	2	8	42	34	22
Glentoran	20	7	2	11	54	56	16
Derry City	20	6	3	11	32	51	15
Cliftonville	20	3	2	15	26	70	8

Regional League 1943–4

	P	W	D	L	F	A	Pts
Belfast Celtic	19	12	5	2	55	21	29

Linfield	18	11	3	4	57	38	25
Distillery	20	10	3	7	52	47	23
Glentoran	20	8	1	11	49	50	17
Cliftonville	20	5	1	14	29	51	11
Derry City	19	5	1	13	35	70	11

Linfield *v* Belfast Celtic and Derry City *v* Linfield not played.

Regional League 1944–5

	P	W	D	L	F	A	Pts
Linfield	20	15	4	1	81	24	34
Belfast Celtic	*20*	*13*	*5*	*2*	*54*	*27*	*31*
Derry City	20	8	3	9	41	53	19
Distillery	20	8	1	11	44	58	17
Glentoran	20	7	1	12	55	67	15
Cliftonville	20	2	0	18	23	69	4

Regional League 1945–6

	P	W	D	L	F	A	Pts
Linfield	20	17	0	3	79	27	34
Belfast Celtic	*20*	*14*	*4*	*2*	*58*	*20*	*32*
Distillery	20	7	5	8	47	52	19
Glentoran	20	5	6	9	46	58	16
Derry City	20	5	1	14	48	72	11
Cliftonville	20	2	4	14	24	73	8

Regional League 1946–7

	P	W	D	L	F	A	Pts
Belfast Celtic	*28*	*21*	*2*	*5*	*95*	*40*	*44*
Glentoran	28	20	2	6	95	46	42
Linfield	28	20	1	7	93	45	41
Coleraine	28	10	5	13	54	75	25
Ballymena United	28	8	7	13	52	76	23
Distillery	28	9	2	17	59	69	20
Derry City	28	9	2	17	53	80	20
Cliftonville	28	3	3	22	46	114	9

The Irish League was restored in season 1947–8.

Season 1947–8

	P	W	D	L	F	A	Pts
Belfast Celtic	*22*	*19*	*1*	*2*	*84*	*26*	*39*
Linfield	22	15	5	2	55	19	35
Ballymena United	22	10	7	5	52	38	27
Distillery	22	12	2	8	35	32	26
Glentoran	22	9	8	5	44	29	26
Coleraine	22	8	6	8	48	46	22
Glenavon	22	8	6	8	45	45	22
Ards	22	7	4	11	39	59	18
Cliftonville	22	7	4	11	36	47	18
Bangor	22	6	4	12	34	50	16
Portadown	22	3	3	16	31	60	9
Derry City	22	2	2	18	18	70	6

Season 1948–9

	P	W	D	L	F	A	Pts
Linfield	22	16	4	2	58	21	36
Belfast Celtic	*22*	*14*	*3*	*5*	*69*	*32*	*31*
Glentoran	22	13	3	6	45	28	29
Cliftonville	22	9	5	8	44	38	23
Bangor	22	8	5	9	43	45	21
Distillery	22	9	3	10	51	56	21
Portadown	22	8	4	10	41	48	20
Glenavon	22	6	8	8	35	43	20
Derry City	22	8	3	11	39	58	19
Ballymena United	22	6	7	9	40	52	19
Ards	22	7	2	13	46	49	16
Coleraine	22	4	1	17	25	66	9

THIRTEEN

THE FINAL SEASON

P re-season predictions indicated that Belfast Celtic and Linfield were going to be the strongest teams in the Irish League in 1948–9. Celtic had a new signing, Gerry McAloon, from Glasgow Celtic, ready to help them in the defence of the City Cup competition.

Belfast Celtic played 38 competitive games in its last season. It won 26 of these, drew seven and lost five. The team scored 115 goals and conceded 46.

SATURDAY, 21 AUGUST 1948

City Cup	Derry 1	Belfast Celtic 6
	Cannon	Jones (3)
		Bonnar
		McMillan
		McAloon

Celtic kicked off the season in style. Jimmy Jones scored a hat-trick, while Paddy Bonnar, Gerry McAloon and Billy McMillan with a direct free kick, completed the scoring. Johnny Campbell did not play in the game because of an injury picked up while representing the Irish League against the touring US Olympic team.

TUESDAY, 25 AUGUST 1948

Gold Cup	Belfast Celtic 2	Glentoran 1
	Denver	Kerr
	McAloon	

Spectators numbering 20,000 packed into Paradise to watch the holders go through to the next round of the Gold Cup competition – Celtic's goalkeeper Kevin McAlinden made a mistake to give the Glens the lead when he was unable to hold Kerr's shot. Denver levelled before half-time and McAloon scored the winner with a header from a Walker free kick.

Jimmy Jones went off injured for ten minutes before resuming in the Celtic attack. Later an X-ray at the Mater Hospital revealed that Jones had a fractured lower jaw and was expected to be out of action for several weeks.

SATURDAY, 28 AUGUST 1948

City Cup   Belfast Celtic 3   Distillery 0

Campbell
McAloon (2)

John Campbell, who replaced Jimmy Jones for the visit of the Whites to Paradise, put the home side on the road to victory with a rasping shot. McAloon's header from a Bonnar cross, 20 minutes from the end, made it 2–0 and the recent signing from Scotland got the third in the closing minutes.

SATURDAY, 4 SEPTEMBER 1948

City Cup   Glentoran 1   Belfast Celtic 1

McFarlane   Graham

This game was played at Grosvenor Park where an Alex Graham equaliser, late in the game, cancelled out McFarlane's goal in the 20th minute. Graham had replaced the injured McAloon and Johnny Campbell was playing at centre-forward. Within minutes of Campbell moving out to the wing and Graham switching to attack, Celtic scrambled the draw.

Bud Aherne failed a fitness test and missed his second game. Reggie Simpson deputised at left-back.

Thursday, 9 September 1948

Gold Cup   Cliftonville 0   Belfast Celtic 1

McAloon

Reggie Simpson again covered for the injured Aherne, while Jimmy Jones, who had fractured his lower jaw less than two weeks previously, was named in the panel and played. Jones set up the winner for McAloon in the 80th minute. George Hazlett replaced the injured Paddy Bonnar.

Saturday, 11 September 1948

City Cup   Belfast Celtic 4   Portadown 0

Jones (2)
McMillan (pen.)
Denver

Jimmy Jones opened the scoring with a header from McAloon's cross and then added a second with a shot.

In the second half, Billy McMillan converted a penalty kick after Portadown defender Woods was judged to have handled the ball. Johnny Denver, who was still struggling to reach full fitness after last season's injury, added the fourth.

Saturday, 18 September 1948

City Cup   Cliftonville 0   Belfast Celtic 6

Jones (3)
Campbell
Denver
Hazlett

Belfast Celtic's second visit to Solitude within a fortnight proved to be much more rewarding when Jones set the pattern for the game with a first-half hat-trick.

Johnny Campbell, Johnny Denver and George Hazlett scored in the second half.

After the game, the Irish League squad left for Liverpool for a game with the Football League.

The Football League won that encounter at Anfield 5–1 on Monday, 20 September 1948. Jimmy Jones scored for the Irish League team which included four players from Belfast Celtic.

Saturday, 25 September 1948

City Cup   Belfast Celtic 5   Coleraine 1

Jones (3)   Clarke

McMillan (pen.)
Hazlett

Coleraine were reduced to ten men when goalkeeper Wright suffered a broken arm, diving at a Jimmy Jones close range shot. Former Celtic star Peter O'Connor went into the Coleraine goal. The visitors took the lead before Jones notched up his third hat-trick of the season. Billy McMillan added a penalty in the second half and Hazlett scored the fourth late in the game.

There was a clash between O'Connor and Paddy Bonnar when the Celtic winger tried to kick the ball out of the hands of the stand-in keeper.

Saturday, 2 October 1948

City Cup   Belfast Celtic 4   Glenavon 1

Jones (3)   Moore
Denver

In this rehearsal for the Gold Cup semi-final, Celtic were rarely under any sustained pressure. Jimmy Jones got the first of his hat-tricks after 12 minutes. Johnny Denver claimed the second when Celtic were awarded an indirect free kick – a new regulation – inside the penalty area. As Glenavon debated the decision, Harry Walker played the ball to the unmarked Denver who easily scored. Jones made it 3–0 before the interval when he was set up by Hazlett and Bonnar to flick the ball past Glenavon goalkeeper Patty.

Alex Moore pulled the game back to 3–1 in the second half before Jones got his third of the afternoon, racing through the centre to score.

Joe Douglas replaced Robin Lawler, who was down with flu.

Saturday, 16 October 1948

City Cup	Ards 3	Belfast Celtic 3
	Booth	Bonnar(2)
	Connor	Campbell
	Corbett	

Belfast Celtic were lucky to survive unbeaten at Castlereagh Park where it required a late strike from Johnny Campbell to force a draw.

Celtic retained Joe Douglas at left-half, while Campbell was brought in at outside-right instead of George Hazlett.

Jones almost claimed the opening goal after 20 minutes, but his drive was blocked by Ards keeper O'Connell, and Bonnar lashed in the rebound.

Booth levelled for Ards on 32 minutes and then set up Connor a minute later to give the home side a 2–1 advantage.

On the stroke of half-time, Bonnar scored his, and Celtic's second, when O'Connell was unable to hold on to a fierce shot and the goalkeeper could only watch as the ball spun across the line.

In the second half, Corbett put Ards in front again and they appeared to be on the way to a surprise win when Campbell salvaged a point which Celtic did not deserve.

Wednesday, 20 October 1948

Gold Cup	Belfast Celtic 1	Glenavon 2
	Bonnar	McLafferty (pen.)
		Moore

Belfast Celtic's first defeat of the season was suffered at Grosvenor Park in the semi-final of the Gold Cup.

The holders were behind within a minute when Charlie Currie was judged to have held Moore back inside the area and McLafferty's penalty was blasted past Kevin McAlinden.

Paddy Bonnar was in the right place to touch in the equaliser on 13 minutes as Glenavon goalkeeper Patty could only parry a shot from Campbell into the path of the in-rushing winger.

Glenavon regained the lead five minutes after half-time when Moore capitalised on a rare error by Harry Walker and scored.

The chances were there for Belfast Celtic to win the game. Firstly, Billy McMillen fired a penalty kick straight at Patty after Cronin had handled, and in injury-time Campbell had the simplest of tasks to force a replay, but he shot wide.

Saturday, 23 October 1948

City Cup   Belfast Celtic 3   Bangor 1

                Campbell   Bradford
                McAloon
                Denver

This was a scrappy game in which Campbell put the home side ahead on the quarter hour. Bradford made it 1–1 with a header from a Gibson cross and then Cunningham had a goal disallowed for the Seasiders.

Belfast Celtic wrapped up the victory in the last 15 minutes. McAloon scored and then set up Denver, who managed to force the ball untidily over the line.

Saturday, 30 October 1948

City Cup   Belfast Celtic 2   Linfield 1

                McAloon   Bryson (pen.)
                Bonnar

This important victory for Belfast Celtic at Paradise broke Linfield's unbeaten run for the season. Gerry McAloon put the Celts in front early in the first half, when he slipped his marker and collected a pass from Jones which was flicked past Alec Russell.

Linfield centre-half Bob Bryson brought the Blues back into the game within a minute from a penalty kick.

Paddy Bonnar supplied the winning goal on 73 minutes by timing his jump perfectly to head a lob from Aherne past Russell.

Celtic might have had a third goal but Robin Lawler's effort was disallowed.

Charlie Currie played a sound game in the Celtic defence and rarely let Linfield centre-forward Billy Simpson out of his sight.

Saturday, 13 November 1948

City Cup   Ballymena 0   Belfast Celtic 3

McAloon
Bonnar
Campbell

Celtic secured the City Cup with this win at the Showgrounds.
McAloon, who saw one effort come back off the woodwork, fired Celtic in front on 37 minutes. Bonnar made it 2–0 after 77 minutes with one of his powerful shots which McCann, the Ballymena keeper, was unable to hold.

Campbell got the third on 86 minutes to make amends for missing a penalty when Jones was hauled down inside the area.

Belfast Celtic retained the City Cup with this victory. A draw would have been sufficient.

City Cup Table

	P	W	D	L	F	A	Pts
Belfast Celtic	*11*	*9*	*2*	*0*	*40*	*9*	*20*
Linfield	11	8	2	1	33	16	18
Portadown	11	7	1	3	27	21	15
Glenavon	11	5	4	2	29	19	14
Glentoran	11	5	3	3	26	17	13
Ards	11	4	1	6	22	23	9
BallymenaUnited	11	4	1	6	20	27	9
Derry City	11	4	1	6	22	31	9
Bangor	11	4	0	7	23	35	8
Distillery	11	3	1	7	20	31	7
Cliftonville	11	2	1	8	11	29	5
Coleraine	11	1	3	7	16	31	5

Saturday, 20 November 1948

Irish League	Glentoran 0	Belfast Celtic 0

The opening game of this season's Irish League Championship ended scoreless at Grosvenor Park.

Saturday, 27 November 1948

Irish League	Belfast Celtic 5	Portadown 1
	Jones (4)	Arthur
	Hazlett	

Portadown, unbeaten in five games, came badly unstuck at Celtic Park. The Ports could have taken the lead early in the game but Brown's shot came off the upright with McAlinden well beaten.

Jones grabbed his first two goals of the game in the 16th and 26th minutes. The first was a tricky shot fired from an awkward angle and the second was struck with such force that Portadown goalkeeper Bennie was left helpless to respond.

George Hazlett added the third almost from the restart and Jones's second double of the afternoon was completed on 52 and 60 minutes.

Arthur hit Portadown's consolation score midway through the second half.

Saturday, 4 December 1948

Irish League	Belfast Celtic 3	Bangor 0
	Jones (2)	
	Campbell	

Belfast Celtic should have won this game by many more goals and were guilty of several missed chances.

Jones put them in front on 9 minutes from close range and slammed home the second before the interval to finish off a move started by Aherne and McAloon.

In the second half, Campbell made it 3–0 as he beat three players to put the ball past Doak.

Saturday, 11 December 1948

Irish League   Derry City 4   Belfast Celtic 3

Aiken   Jones (2)
Gilmartin   (2)   Denver
Colvin

A defensive misunderstanding between Harry Walker and Robin Lawler allowed Derry City's Colvin in to score the winning goal, two minutes from time, in this seven-goal thriller.

Derry went in front after 25 minutes with a clever header by Aiken and were two ahead shortly afterwards, when the unmarked Gilmartin finished off Kelly's free kick.

Jones pulled one back after the interval and then Colvin and Gilmartin created Derry's 3–1 lead – the latter claiming the final touch.

Denver and Jones became more effective in the Celtic attack and when Denver reduced the score to 3–2, Jones powered through for the equaliser with a shot from outside the penalty area which left Derry keeper McCann stranded.

Celtic, playing below par, were inhibited by an injury which left Campbell moving at half pace. Worse was to follow when Bud Aherne failed to reappear after the interval because of a groin injury picked up early in the game.

However Derry, without a win in the Championship until this display, were worthy winners of a match played in heavy conditions underfoot.

The defeat – only Celtic's second of the season – left Linfield as the one remaining unbeaten team in the League.

Saturday, 18 December 1948

Irish League   Belfast Celtic 4   Coleraine 0

Jones (3)
Denver

Even without the services of the injured Aherne, McAloon and Campbell, Belfast Celtic coasted to an easy victory against the

Bannsiders. Jones, who scored a hat-trick, wasted three times as many chances and could have surpassed Peter O'Connor's record 11 goals against Glenavon in 1941.

Denver got the fourth goal.

Reggie Simpson, playing at full-back in place of Aherne, limped off 20 minutes from the end and there was a very impressive display from Broadway man Tommy Tucker who was selected instead of McAloon.

Saturday, 25 December 1948

Irish League	Ballymena 0	Belfast Celtic 5
		Hazlett
		Jones
		Denver (2)
		McMillan

Kevin McAlinden was rested for this game at the Showgrounds and Oswald Bailie, who deputised in goal, was rarely tested.

George Hazlett opened the scoring after 6 minutes and Jones headed in a Bonnar cross in the 35th minute to give Celtic a 2–0 lead at the interval. Denver scored twice in the second half and McMillan added the fifth in the final minute with a 30-yard free kick.

Season 1948-9 League Table

	P	W	D	L	F	A	Pts
Linfield	6	6	0	0	20	4	12
Belfast Celtic	6	4	1	1	20	5	9
Glentoran	6	3	2	2	16	8	8
Cliftonville	6	3	1	1	14	7	7
Bangor	6	3	1	2	17	14	7
Portadown	6	3	1	2	14	13	7
Derry City	6	2	1	3	11	15	5
Ballymena United	6	2	1	3	12	19	5
Distillery	6	2	0	4	12	17	4
Ards	6	1	1	4	10	19	3
Glenavon	6	1	1	4	8	19	3
Coleraine	6	1	0	5	1	20	2

Monday, 27 December 1948

Irish League　　　　　Linfield 1　　　　　Belfast Celtic 1

Simpson　　　　　Walker (pen.)

Belfast Celtic went into this Boxing Day fixture at Windsor Park trailing the League leaders Linfield by three points. As the League table indicates, Celtic needed to win to pressurise Linfield who were reduced to ten men when Bryson was carried off with a suspected broken ankle in the first half of a very tense match.

Linfield lost another player when Jackie Russell took the full force of a Celtic clearance and had to leave the field. In the 72nd minute, Albert Currie was sent off by referee Norman Boal for deliberately fouling Paddy Bonnar and moments later, Bonnar was also dismissed for verbally abusing the linesman.

Harry Walker's penalty kick gave Celtic the lead with ten minutes remaining after McCune was adjudged to have brought down Denver inside the area.

Linfield, however, pulled an equaliser out of nothing with a few minutes left on the watch. Billy Simpson fired in a shot which gave McAlinden no chance to save and that signalled a pitch invasion. The restart was delayed while the crowd was cleared, but they returned in a more vicious mood as the final whistle sounded. Several of the Celtic players including McAlinden, Hazlett, Walker, Lawler and Jones were attacked. Jones suffered a multiple-fracture of the right leg.

The police made no arrests.

Saturday, 1 January 1949

Irish League　　　　　Belfast Celtic 3　　　　　Glenavon 1

Denver　　　　　Moore
Walker (2, pen.)

Absent from the Celtic team were McAlinden, Lawler and of course Jones. Denver was set up for the opening goal with a pass by Hazlett which he finished off with a rising drive into the roof of the net.

Walker converted a penalty kick for a hand ball offence before the interval and made it 3–0 in the second half. Moore scored Glenavon's consolation goal with a well-placed header past the grasp of Bailie.

Saturday, 8 January 1949

Irish League	Belfast Celtic 10	Distillery 2
	Campbell (6)	Mullholland (2)
	Denver (2)	
	Bonnar	
	Hazlett	

Distillery were completely outplayed in the heavy conditions at Celtic Park where Campbell, restored to the centre-forward position, was a revelation.

Campbell notched up five on the way to Celtic's record-achieving first-half tally of eight goals. Denver scored twice and Bonnar the other.

In the second half, Bonnar, who had an outstanding game, continued to provide the service from the wing as Campbell got his sixth, and Hazlett, who should have had more, made it ten. As Celtic relaxed at the back, Mulholland hit two late replies for the Whites.

Saturday, 15 January 1949

Irish League	Cliftonville 2	Belfast Celtic 5
	Black	Campbell (2)
	McGarry	McAloon (2)
		Bonnar

Celtic survived some early pressure from Cliftonville at Solitude to take the lead on ten minutes. Former Celtic forward McGarry had an effort cleared off the line by Charlie Currie and, in the Celtic counter-attack, Bonnar's cross was deflected into the path of Campbell by Barnes, and the centre-forward fired past Reid.

McAloon scored twice in the half to leave Celtic 3–1 in front. Black replied for the home side. Campbell made it 4–1 with a precision header before McGarry got a second for the home side.

Bonnar was in top form in this game and his positional sense played a large part in his goal when Hazlett provided him with the simplest of tap-ins. The 1,200-seater Cliftonville Stand was burned down later in the evening. The wooden stand and its tar roof were destroyed. Firemen believed the blaze may have been started by a smouldering cigarette.

SATURDAY, 22 JANUARY 1949

Irish Cup	Portadown 1	Belfast Celtic 0
	Wood	

Belfast Celtic crashed out of the Irish Cup when Portadown left-half Wood scored the only goal of the tie at Shamrock Park with 20 minutes left to play.

Celtic goalkeeper Josh Sloan failed to hold a centre and, as the ball broke free, Aherne cleared the danger to concede a corner kick. But the Celtic defence were all at sea as Wood rose higher than the rest to power a header into the net.

Portadown took advantage of the absence of key Celtic players Jones – injured – and Bonnar – suspended – to book their place in the next round.

SATURDAY, 29 JANUARY 1949

Irish League	Belfast Celtic 4	Ards 3
	Walker (3, pen.)	Sloan
	Campbell	Smyth
		Case

Ards appeared to be on course for a shock victory at Celtic Park when Harry Walker played the captain's role and, leading by example, forced the home side back into contention.

Ards took the lead in the second minute through Sloan and made it 2–0 on 55 minutes as a McMillan slip-up was punished by the accurate finishing of Smyth.

Ten minutes later, Ards appeared to have an unassailable lead when Currie, caught in two minds whether to clear the ball or pass it back, did neither and let Case in to score and make it 3–0.

But Walker's 16 years of experience was brought into immediate action as he switched to centre-forward and pulled a goal back from the kick-off. Minutes later Walker slotted home a penalty kick following a hand ball offence by Dunne.

Celtic, scenting an equaliser, continued to pressurise the Ards back line and Walker set up Campbell to level the game from Hazlett's cross ball. The winning goal came a short time later when Walker completed his hat-trick inside the space of 12 minutes with a well-placed shot.

Former Antrim Gaelic football star Harry O'Neill, making his debut for Celtic, never got to grips with the flow of the game.

Saturday, 5 February 1949

Irish League	Glentoran 3	Belfast Celtic 0
	Lavery	
	McFarlane	
	Kerr	

Glentoran half-backs, Hughes and Blanchflower, were in total control of the game, keeping the Celtic inside-forwards at bay. But Walker and Lawler never got to grips as Glentoran continued to push the ball forward to McFarlane and Kerr via Feeney on the left wing.

McMillan was unable to contain the winger who set up Glentoran's three goals – all scored in the first half.

Lavery was the first on target on the quarter hour as he fired past Bailie from close range when Kerr headed the ball into his path.

McFarlane had the easiest of tasks to score the second after 21 minutes. Feeney was given lots of space and time to pick out the centre-forward who stabbed the ball past the Celtic goalkeeper, Bailie.

Glentoran's third goal on the stroke of half-time was again created from play down the left wing, though Celtic's defence claimed that Kerr was in an offside position when he received the ball. Johnny Denver did have the ball in the Glentoran net on two occasions, but both were disallowed.

Elisha Scott's tactical change of switching Walker to centre-forward and Denver to outside-right, failed to produce any dividends.

Saturday, 19 February 1949

Irish League	Portadown 2	Belfast Celtic 4
	Mullet	Hazlett
	Brown	Silcock
		Denver (2)

Celtic's performance in this League encounter was a hundred times better than in the recent Irish Cup defeat at Shamrock Park. The visitors were not too perturbed when Mullet gave the Ports an early lead.

Johnny Denver jinxed his way through the home defence in the space of two minutes to equalise, and then give Celtic the lead. New boy George Silcock from Lurgan made his mark on the game with his first goal and Hazlett added the fourth before Brown hit back for Portadown close to the end.

Jimmy Jones was a spectator at the game and it was made known that his chances of playing next season were very remote. Meanwhile it was reported that Linfield centre-half Bob Bryson, who was injured in the Boxing Day game, was due to have his plaster removed shortly.

Saturday, 26 February 1949

Irish League	Bangor 0	Belfast Celtic 1
		Morrison

Bangor, in advance of the Irish Cup with Derry, played five reserves. Belfast Celtic should have won by much more, but for wasted chances by Denver.

The only goal was scored by Vincent Morrison who scrambled the ball over the line after Hazlett had worked a passage up the right wing and crossed the ball unchallenged.

Saturday, 5 March 1949

Irish League   Belfast Celtic 8   Derry City 0

Campbell (2)
Silcock (5)
Morrison

This game at Celtic park was one-way traffic from the moment that Johnny Campbell gave the home side the lead in the opening minutes. Campbell might have scored more than his two, had the playing surface not cut up so badly in the winter conditions.

Morrison, the match-winner last time against Bangor, got on the score sheet again, while Silcock scored the first of his five.

Celtic were 4–0 in front at the interval and the second half virtually belonged to Silcock who scored three in the space of 12 minutes.

Silcock and Morrison operating on the right side of attack blended together more effectively than Hazlett and Denver.

Saturday, 12 March 1949

Irish League   Coleraine 1   Belfast Celtic 0

Hamill

Belfast Celtic dropped valuable League points in this surprise defeat at the Showgrounds. The absence of Campbell was obvious as the visiting attack failed to ignite.

Coleraine scored the only goal of the game after ten minutes when Hamill headed in O'Reilly's corner kick.

Saturday, 19 March 1949

Irish League   Belfast Celtic 3   Ballymena 2

Morrison   McDonald
Bonnar (2, pen.)   Williamson

Paddy Bonnar played for the first time since serving his eight-week suspension and scored twice in Celtic's 3–2 win at home to Ballymena.

Morrison gave Celtic the lead after 20 minutes from Bonnar's left-wing centre. Bonnar showed a remarkable turn of speed to put Celtic 2–0 in front from the restart and then converted a penalty kick after Jackson handled.

Ballymena fought back with goals from McDonald and Williamson and were left to rue a missed penalty in the first half by Cronin.

Saturday, 26 March 1949

Irish League	Ards 4	Belfast Celtic 4
	Magennis (2)	Denver (2)
	Case	Bradford (2)
	Smyth	

Celtic were trailing 4–0 at the interval and, as in the previous meeting between the two clubs, Harry Walker's side clawed its way back from defeat.

In that game on 29 January, Walker had secured victory with a hat-trick in the 4–3 result, but this time Celtic had to be satisfied with a point.

Denver, who had lost the scoring touch in recent weeks, fired in two precious goals in the second half, while Bradford, Celtic's recent signing from Bangor, was on hand to help snatch the draw.

Saturday, 2 April 1949

Irish League	Belfast Celtic 0	Linfield 1
		Simpson

In the first meeting of Belfast Celtic and Linfield since the Boxing Day game of 1948, this tense affair at Celtic Park produced a single goal and a victory for Linfield. The result virtually assured the Blues of the Irish League title.

Simpson, who had been well marshalled throughout the game by Charlie Currie, got a snap chance for a shot on target and he took it gratefully, ten minutes into the second half.

Belfast Celtic did have the ball in the net when Currie hit a magnificent 25-yard drive past Jack Russell in the Linfield goal. Unfortunately the referee judged Bonnar to be offside – though home fans argued that he was not interfering with play.

Tuesday, 5 April 1949

County Antrim Shield	Belfast Celtic 2	Ards 1
	Morgan (2)	Magennis

This game, which Celtic won easily, marked the return to action of long-term injury victim Kevin McAlinden in the Celtic goalkeeping position.

Saturday, 9 April 1949

Irish League	Glenavon 1	Belfast Celtic 0
	Kelly	

Glenavon winger Kelly scored on the hour in a curious game in which the goalkeepers had little to do, though both sets of forwards missed several chances.

Tuesday, 19 April 1949

Irish League	Belfast Celtic 2	Distillery 1
	Denver (2)	Kirkpatrick

Celtic completed a hat-trick of victories over their near neighbours with this 2–1 win at Celtic Park.

Johnny Denver got both goals for the home side – the first after 17 minutes when the Celtic forward got in behind the Distillery defence to stab the ball past Smyth.

Two minutes later Denver finished neatly again, this time from a tentative lob into the penalty area by Joe Douglas.

Distillery scored through Kirkpatrick with 20 minutes remaining and Blackledge almost grabbed a late equaliser – but McAlinden made a fine save.

Thursday, 21 April 1949

Irish League	Belfast Celtic 4	Cliftonville 3
	McMillan (2)	McGarry (2)
	Walker	Magill
	Hazlett	

Belfast Celtic's final game at Celtic Park ended with a 4-3 win over Cliftonville, who held the lead at half-time through a McGarry goal.

Walker levelled the game early in the second half before a McMillan free kick put the home side in front. McMillan scored again and Hazlett made it 4–2 before McGarry and Magill scored for the Reds.

BIBLIOGRAPHY

The History of Irish Soccer, Malcolm Brodie, Arrell Publications 1962.

Football Association of Ireland – 75 Years, Peter Byrne, Sportsworld Publication 1996.

Dreams, and Songs to Sing: A New History of Celtic, Tom Campbell & Pat Woods, Mainstream Publishing Co. 1996.

Belfast Celtic, John Kennedy, Pretani Press 1989.

The Story of Celtic 1888–1938, Willie Maley, Desert Island Football History 1996.

Passed to You, Charlie Tully, Stanley Paul 1958.

Belfast Celtic, Mark Tuohy, Blackstaff Press 1978.